D0152667

Money and Democracy

Money & Democracy

George Macesich

PRAEGER

New York
Westport, Connecticut
London

Library of Congress Cataloging-in-Publication Data

Macesich, George, 1927–
Money and democracy / George Macesich.
p. cm.
Includes bibliographical references.
ISBN 0–275–93480–2 (alk. paper)
1. Money—United States. 2. Monetary policy—United States.
I. Title.
HG501.M33 1990
332.4'973—dc20 89–26540

Library of Congress Catalog Card Number: 89–26540
ISBN: 0–275–93480–2

First published in 1990

Praeger Publishers, One Madison Avenue, New York, NY 10010
An imprint of Greenwood Publishing Group, Inc.

Printed in the United States of America

∞

The paper used in this book complies with the Permanent Paper Standard issued by the National Information Standards Organization (Z39.48–1984).

10 9 8 7 6 5 4 3 2 1

To the memory of
Walter Macesich, Jr.
1928–1988

Contents

Tables

Acknowledgments

I am indebted to Milton Friedman, Anna J. Schwartz, Marshall R. Colberg, Walter Macesich, Jr. and other colleagues with whom I have in the past discussed one or another aspect of this study. I should also like to express appreciation to Esther C. S. Glenn for editorial assistance and to Tammy Sexton for wordprocessing services.

Introduction

There is general agreement that no problem has encountered more diversity of interpretation in democracies than the theory of money and monetary policy. The debates seem endless, but they boil down to one issue: how best to consider money, monetary policy and the monetary regime against the widespread argument for a liberal, freely functioning trading world and for fully employed, prosperous member countries.

Can a democratic market system based on self-interest be entrusted to an unconstrained bureaucracy and political elite? Can an enlightened elite of bureaucratic managers realistically be expected to suppress their individual interest for the general interest? Can they manage a monetary standard within a majoritarian democracy so as to anchor the long-term price level? Can a democracy and market economy survive if they fail?

The facts are that the authority of the state and its bureaucratic apparatus including monetary authorities has increased, presumably to provide satisfactory solutions to these problems. This expansion has been expedient but inglorious, necessary but dangerous, useful but costly. Along with this expansion has been renewed concern over the moral and social values underpinning the democratic market system. This has promoted renewed discussion of various theses regarding the viability of market society.[1]

Professor J. R. Hicks tells us that in his search for a workable monetary standard, John Maynard Keynes found in the *General Theory* the labor standard and its dependence on society's sociopolitical processes.[2] This, in turn, translated into, among other things, a "managed monetary standard" and justification for its discretionary management by central monetary authorities composed of an "enlightened elite."

Keynes, of course, was well aware of the precariousness of efforts to calculate the course of human affairs.[3] Man constructs institutions and arrangements which give the illusion of rational foresight and stability. General breakdowns do occur from time to time for that is also the course of human events. With breakdowns come shattered illusions. Thus it is, for instance, that with breakdowns employment and enterprise suffer because decision makers seek refuge for their reserves of wealth in money itself.

The human institution of money which serves as a vehicle for man's endless journey into an uncertain future can thus be a source of disturbance by serving as a refuge for wealth. Indeed, Keynes' *General Theory* for the most part deals with the circumstances and institutions and particularly the institution of money which man has built in his attempts to make the uncertain certain.

Long before Keynes, Georg Simmel in his *Philosophy of Money* underscores that an "unmanaged" or "free" monetary order was cast in doubt.[4] He identifies two likely sources of trouble for a free monetary order. One source is that since individuals do not receive income in kind but rather in money, they are exposed to the uncertainties originating in fluctuations in the purchasing power of money. The other is that the very success of a free monetary order encourages the development of socialist or collectivist ideas which serve to undermine the individualistic order based on free markets and money.

The existence of a growing body of evidence on the vote-maximizing behavior of politicians and politically induced cycles in such key variables as inflation, unemployment, government transfers, taxes and monetary growth suggests the critical nature of the problem in democracy.

The appeal to central authority that the problem produces was discussed long ago by that shrewd observer of American democracy, Alexis de Tocqueville.[5] He warned that in the first half of the nineteenth century democracy could falter as a consequence of citizens' diminished interest in restraining central authority. He noted that since democratic man would not be able to count on his neighbors for support he had an incentive to increase the power of the central authority. He was in a sense predicting the rise of the protective welfare state.

As a matter of fact the American founders did not really expect people to become absorbed in politics and public affairs because they themselves experienced politics as unpleasant, intrusive and undignified. Whatever the founders may have felt about civic duty, they clearly did not feel that politics answered to man's higher nature. James Madison not only distrusted but dreaded "interested majorities." Indeed he followed David Hume in demonstrating that liberty is best safeguarded in an expansive political territory because here the diversity of interests and attitudes precludes unity of popular action.

Their project, the federal Constitution, is an exercise in constructing a government out of defective human parts. They believed that the urge to tyrannize others was so strong that external restraints became absolutely indispensable. The image of man in their discourse appears less than free and rational because his will and intelligence may be at the service of his "passions," forces beyond himself that make self-control improbable.[6] In both Federalist and anti-Federalist political factions a vague egalitarianism also led to the fear of elitism, "the artful and ever active aristocracy" usurping the power that belonged to an unalert and passive people, and Walter Lippmann put it succinctly when he informed Americans that the framers of the Constitution bequeathed to future generations of Americans a government of checks and balances.

The skepticism of the founders toward the general public appears well founded even 200 years later. To judge by recent (1988) surveys of American high school students conducted by the Joint Council on Economic Education students get failing marks. Just 34 percent of those seniors surveyed were correct on national economic questions and 36 percent on international questions. Furthermore, only 25 percent could define inflation and fewer than 30 percent recognized that a lack of labor skills was a major cause of low income. Economic literacy has a wide effect on how well people are able to survive in society as consumers, as workers, and as citizens. Certainly these results do not inspire confidence that the general public is capable of dealing on equal terms with the maximizing behavior of an "artful and ever active" bureaucracy and political elite.[7]

This study supports the view that constraints must be placed on the exercise of discretionary authority by vote-maximizing bureaucracies and political elites if democracy is to thrive and prosper.[8] Satisfactory resolution to these issues is basic to reducing monetary uncertainty and stabilizing the long-term price level. These issues are deeply embedded in traditional American ideology and experience. This is perhaps best illustrated as in this study in the case of money and monetary policy by weaving together historical, institutional, theoretical, philosophical, and empirical results so each reinforces the other. It is only when these many strands are woven together that we have better insight into the issues involved in the on-going debate over money, monetary policy and the monetary regime in democratic societies.

NOTES

1. For discussion of four conflicting theses about the market society see Albert Hirschman, "Rival Interpretations of Market Society: Civilizing, Destructive, or Feeble?" *Journal of Economic Literature*, December, 1982. pp. 1463–84.

2. J. R. Hicks, "The Keynes Centenary: A Skeptical Follower." *The Economist*, June 18, 1983. pp. 17–19; J. M. Keynes, *The General Theory of Employment, Interest and Money* (New York: Harcourt, Brace and World, 1964).

3. G. L. S. Shackle, *The Years of High Theory: Invention and Tradition in Economic Thought, 1926–1939* (Cambridge: Cambridge University Press, 1983): pp. 149ff.

4. Georg Simmel, *The Philosophy of Money*. Translation by T. Bottomore and D. Frisby. With Introduction by D. Frisby. (London and Boston: Rutledge and Kegan Paul, 1977, 1978). This study was first published in German in 1907.

5. Alexis de Tocqueville, *Democracy in America* (Garden City, NY: Doubleday, 1969).

6. For a discussion of these issues, see J. P. Diggins, *The Lost Soul of American Politics: Virtue, Self-Interest, and the Foundations of Liberalism* (New York: Basic Books, 1984) and Joyce Appleby, *Capitalism and a New Social Order: The Republican Vision of the 1790's* (New York: New York University Press, 1984).

7. Much of the basic contributions to our understanding of these pro-

cesses are from the work of Professor James M. Buchanan, Nobel prize winner, and his associates in public choice theory.

8. The contributions by Professor Milton Friedman are, of course, the basic studies for our understanding of these issues.

Money and Democracy

Chapter 1

Monetary Problems in Democracy

THE ISSUES

Monetary problems in democracy are as fascinating as they are perplexing, combining as they do a rich mixture of technical economics, interactions of political and economic factors, and even the psychology of symbols and beliefs. The various "solutions" have come protected by strong political, economic and ideological interests. In part, the difficulties seem to arise from economic circumstances, theory and methodology of the interwar and postwar periods. Thus group interests and group ideologies remain involved in the discussion, with the Federal Reserve and other central banks joining the banking community and national governments with immense opinion-making resources in a long-standing involvement in these issues.

Central to these issues is the perpetual disagreement over defined versus undefined or discretionary policy systems. On the one side are the monetarists or quantity theorists urging a policy system based on rules and nondiscretionary intervention into the economy. Its principal corollary is that a slow and steady rate of increase in the money supply—one in line with the real growth of the economy—can insure price stability.[1]

On the other side of the issue are people whose preference is administrative intervention to maintain aggregate demand in the economy. They include modern Keynesians and central bankers whose position is that defined policy systems are inferior to administrative discretion.

In effect, the modern Keynesian position and that of central bankers does not involve a search for optimal decision rules for monetary (and fiscal) policy. Central bankers are more or less in accord since it is consistent with their view that the conduct of monetary policy is an "art" not to be encumbered by explicit policy rules.

Essentially, the modern Keynesian approach is the economic branch of the political interventionist position whose defining principle is the extensive use of government power without definite guides or policy systems. It has important allies in central banks with whom it shares many banking school ideas. Its opponents, including monetarists, are those seeking lawful policy systems and limitations on the undefined exercise of power by government. John M. Culbertson puts the issue well when he writes:

> A basic difficulty with undefined policy systems . . . is that since the policies to be followed are uncertain, they may prove to be disastrously inappropriate. Such policy systems are risky. The intellectual difficulty of the proponent of discretionary policy formation is a real one. If the policy matters, then certain correct choices must be made, which implies that power must reside in those particular men who will make the correct decisions—but in a context in which the correct choices themselves are asserted to be incapable of being defined (since it is the basis of rejection of defined policy systems). Inevitably, it seems, the approach implies the existence of an elite or priestly class that promises to accomplish the indefinable.[2]

Money and monetary policy, in effect, become the connecting link between two interacting systems: the economic and political. This chapter focuses on the manner in which this link is accomplished and its implications. It is a critical issue in the on-going problem of macroeconomic stability. It is, moreover, central to the preservation of the market system and political pluralism so basic to Western type economies.[3] It is fundamental to monetary reform.

Thus, the fact that the Keynesian view takes the position that prices and wages are determined outside the system through sociopolitical processes has important implications for our study.[4] These processes constitute, for the most part, an arbitrary exercise of power by bureaucracies and political elites. The power is arbitrary in the sense that its exercise is neither tempered by competitive market forces nor answerable to society as a whole. There is little to assure that under the circumstances the economy will respond appropriately to government manipulation of aggregate demand by monetary and fiscal policies. As a result, government must of necessity participate in the formation of these prices and wages to assure a desired outcome.

This will typically lead to price and wage controls creating or strengthening bureaucracies to administer them. Since wage and price controls inevitably fail, the system is increasingly driven into collective participatory planning where wages and prices are determined. One consequence is to enhance governmental and bureaucratic power and the interests of those whose preference is for the exercise of discretionary power. This will tend to be at the expense of arrangements whereby money and the monetary system are allowed to play a nondiscretionary and autonomous role within the constraints of a rules-based policy system.

The inevitable failure of price and wage controls is readily demonstrated by considering some problems and consequences of controlling prices for goods and services (including wages). The effects of a fixed price for a product or service depend in the first instance on the level at which it is fixed and whether it is a minimum or a maximum price.

To illustrate the issues, let us suppose we set up an administrative agency to fix prices. Now suppose this agency fixed the price of a commodity or service precisely at the level at which it would fall relative to other prices if there were no price controls and the price were established by free market forces. In this case, the price control will have no effect, and our agency will have performed a needless exercise. Of course, the administrative costs incurred by this exercise will be borne by the taxpayer.

Now suppose that our agency sets a fixed price that is a maximum price, but that it sets the price at some level lower than what the price would be if it were determined by free market forces. In this case shortages will appear. People will want to buy more of the commodity or service than they otherwise would, but less of the product or service will be produced or offered than otherwise would have been produced. Why should less of the product be produced at this lower price? The reason is simply that at this lower price it becomes more profitable to produce other items whose prices are not fixed at this lower level. Now if more is demanded than is supplied, then some system determines who among the people is going to get the product or service in question. This can be done by attaching another office to our price-administering agency whose function will be to issue coupons, or the product or service can be given to old and regular customers of the suppliers, or it can be done according to the rule of "first come, first served." This is, of course, the familiar case of the queue with all the losses in time spent waiting one's turn.

If less of a product or service is produced because its price is fixed too low, it must be that fewer resources are employed. Now, what happened to those resources? They simply moved to other industries producing products and services whose prices were not controlled. Ironically, since prices that tend to be controlled in "essential" industries are not controlled in "unessential" industries, this means that price controls tend to cause fewer of the essential products or services to be produced.

The above need not be the case at all, some will say, since the government can induce producers of the commodity or service in question to produce more at this lower price by offering them an incentive in the form of a subsidy. All this means is that, in effect, producers now receive a higher price, raised "artificially" by the government subsidy. The taxpayer in general will now bear not only the cost of the price-administering agency but also the additional cost of the subsidy.

Consider our last case in which a minimum price is fixed at a level higher than that which would prevail in a free market. Now there will be initial surpluses. At a higher price for the product or service, more will be produced. Instead of rationing consumers, it will now be necessary to "ration" the production of the product or service among the many producers who would be willing to produce at this higher price. Again, as in the case of consumers, this can be done by attaching an office to our price-administering agency whose function will be to allocate by quota, production of the product or service in question.

This, in general, is the all-too-familiar problem in the past of U.S. agricultural surpluses. In this case, the taxpayer as a consumer will very likely pay the higher price for the product or service as well as the cost of the administering agency.

Selective price controls, cannot avoid discrimination. If a producer's selling price is fixed, there is usually an obligation to control his costs. This means fixing more than the prices of a producer's more obvious inputs such as labor and raw materials. It also means that such items as taxes, interest costs, and business costs must also be fixed.

Control of labor costs, however, is the most difficult. Elements of labor costs, such as fringe benefits, compensation for overtime work, shift differentials, and paid leave, serve to complicate the already difficult task of setting wage rates. The U.S. federal minimum wage will suffice to illustrate the difficulties in setting wage rates.[5]

The inverse relationship between changes in the minimum wage and substitution (capital for labor) effects one would expect from economic theory appears to be confirmed. When information on evasion and violations of the minimum wage law is taken into account, considerable light is shed on the complexities of wage fixing. In effect, an increase in the minimum wage is equivalent to a reduction in the price of evasion and avoidance. The price of evasion and avoidance is the cost of evasion and avoidance minus the benefits of evasion and avoidance. The benefit has increased with the increase in the minimum wage. Other things being equal, one would expect evasion and avoidance of the minimum wage to increase. This also appears to be confirmed by the evidence.[6]

The minimum wage has had adverse effects on wage differentials,[7] and these differentials serve a useful purpose in allocating labor services into various occupations. They are, in fact, an essential part of the price mechanism. When they are subjected to an autonomous shock in the form of a government fiat, a compression of wage differentials occurs. The wages of those directly affected by the rise in the minimum wage rise more than wages of those not so directly affected. Since it is not as easy to allocate labor services as it is other goods and services, the problem of production adjustments is aggravated.

Matters are further complicated by difficulties in defining exactly what it is that is being controlled. Failure to specify accurately the end product or service leads to the inevitable tendency to increase profit margins by cutting quality, particularly where shortages already exist. The problem, moreover, is not simply one of quality deterioration. There is also the tendency for the variety of products to be reduced.

In the face of domestic price and wage ceilings, there is always the tendency for a producer to sell abroad at a higher price. When the producer is allocated fewer productive resources than he desires, he may seek to increase his supply by imports. This inevitably leads to price controls and import and export quotas. The general direction into which a country adopting such controls is pushed forces its government and bureaucracy into a position as the sole judge of the volume and direction new investment will take. Government, and more specifically its bureaucracy, dominates the field of new investment through its policies regarding profits and sales.

The fundamental truths discussed above are also applicable to foreign exchange markets where central bankers, treasury officials, and other experts regularly intervene or promote one objective or another. The fact is that a fixed or targeted range for currencies in international markets will last only so long as market forces agree with it. Seldom, if ever, have policy-makers been able to outsmart for any extended period the collective judgment of buyers and sellers in markets. Flexible exchange rates, while far from perfect, are the best system to sort out the complexities that make up the relative value of currency.

And indeed American experience since the abandonment of fixed exchange rates supports the view that free market forces thereafter did indeed correctly reflect market forces. Thus the U.S. dollar's value dropped sharply in 1973 and 1980 when the U.S. experienced high inflation and weakened economic conditions. It rose beginning in 1981 when U.S. policies dramatically changed, and the Federal Reserve pursued a vigorous anti-inflationary policy. This record is surely not one of failure on the part of flexible exchange rates or markets.

The dollar's price is not a cause but, rather, a symptom of the problem. It is axiomatic that price is a reflection of a fundamental value in the market. To argue, as some people do, that the high (or low) dollar hurts (or benefits) the U.S. economy does not explain how or why the price got there nor does it prove that the flexible exchange-rate system has failed. Rather, the opposite is true.

An illustration of the exchange-rate interventionist appeal is provided by reaction to U.S. Treasury Secretary James Baker's seven-nation economic coordination plan presented at the Economic Summit in Tokyo, Japan in May, 1986. The seven nations involved were the United States, West Germany, Japan, Great Britain, France, Canada, and Italy. Former Secretary Baker's plan, which called for the respective finance ministers to meet each year to devise a strategy for making their fixed or targeted range for currencies in international markets, will last only so long as market forces agree with it. Seldom, if ever, have policymakers been able to outsmart for any extended period the collective judgment of buyers and sellers in markets.

To critics the principal question remains: How long will it take for the finance ministers to translate the new review mechanism into the kind of economic policy changes that will help stabilize exchange rates? Conflicting goals in key industrial countries, they argue, will not make the task easier. There is nothing in the new mechanism that would make an errant country change its course. In their view, the most important aspect of Secretary Baker's plan is that it underscores that the U.S. administration is prepared after all to take a more activist role reversing the maxim that exchange rates should be left entirely to the market.

No doubt the critics and others who subscribe to interventionist ideas have good intentions in calling for more activist government policies in the market. They may be dedicated to the goal of global prosperity. Unfortunately, they are misguided in believing that this worthy goal can be advanced by reversing the maxim that exchange rates should be left entirely to the market. Intervention, as with every intoxicating elixir, has certain mass appeal. Unfortunately it serves to perpetuate the false belief that policymakers can indeed outsmart the collective judgment of the market.

The point is that observed volatility of exchange rates is but a surface manifestation of more fundamental disturbances in the form of misguided and inappropriate monetary and fiscal policies. If the volatility of these manifestations is not permitted in the foreign exchange market, it will appear elsewhere where it may be very difficult to handle. Fixing or manipulating exchange rates without introducing a significant change in the conduct of policies may not improve matters at all. It is like breaking a thermometer instead of properly regulating the sources of heat in a room.

Partisans of fixed exchange rates typically argue that they impose discipline on governments. Thus when rates seem to be breaking, governments are under pressure to change policies to sustain rates. Postwar experience, particularly since the 1970s, does not support such confidence. Instead of changing policies to stay with the fixed exchange rate system, major industrial countries simply dropped the system.

Even more important, perhaps, failure to allow the market system to play its effective and efficient role almost assures that money and the monetary system will not be allowed to play a nondiscriminatory and autonomous role within the constraints of a rules-based policy system so necessary to assure the preservation of economic and monetary stability in the country.

This outcome may indeed be desired by the bureaucracy and politicians. It is the recognition of such an outcome that prompts the extension of economic analysis to bureaucratic and political analysis. Thus, we have it from the theory of bureaucracy that we can expect central bankers not to take seriously theory and evidence that will constrain their activities. This has little to do with individual central bankers, many of whom are outstanding. At issue is the system itself and the incentives to which central bankers respond.

Central bankers view their conduct of monetary policy as an "art" which leaves the policy system conveniently undefined and open to discretionary control. They will not voluntarily give up their discretionary authority for that of a monetary policy defined and constrained by the behavior of the money supply as urged by monetarists. This is understandable. There is, after all, a problem of power. And power is the ability of its holder to exact compliance or obedience of other individuals to his will on whatever basis.

It is concern for its own power and prestige that prompts an agency such as a central bank to prefer discretionary policy systems. A policy defined and constrained by rules or performance criteria signals less power and prestige. For this reason, it prefers economic theories and models that support discretionary policy systems and shuns those that lead to defined optimal behavior of such instrumental variables as defined money supply functions. Scientific evidence that would lead to the imposition of explicit decision rules that would undermine its power is questioned, evaded or ridiculed. With no "bottom line" or constraint the less likely it is that the agency can be demonstrated to have made serious errors.[8]

Central banks as government agencies exercise discretionary policy. It is important to have an independent evaluation of their performance in terms of explicit criteria. Central banks are loath to accept this constraint, since they view the exercise of monetary policy as an "art" that cannot be defined or measured in terms of any single variable. Their preference is to discuss monetary policy in terms of unmeasured restraint, or else in terms of a set of nonequivalent measuring variables among which the interpreter is free to choose as he wishes.

A LOOK AT THE EVIDENCE

A case in point, illustrating well the issues involved, is the experience cited by Milton Friedman in his exchange with Federal Reserve authorities.[9] In describing a 1969 Federal Reserve conference on controlling monetary aggregates, he writes:

> Prior and subsequent to this time, outside persons were invited to meet with members of the board in Washington from time to time. I attended many such meetings of so-called academic consultants. They were interesting experiences, no doubt instructive to the many Federal Reserve personnel who sat around the sides of the boardroom, where the meeting was invariably held, without participating. However, I finally concluded that the meetings were called purely for window-dressing purposes. I was unable to detect any influence whatsoever exerted by the consultants' comments on the system's actions. Indeed, the choice of the particular consultants invited to attend seemed designed to guarantee offsetting and contradictory advice, leaving the Fed free to pursue its own devices. However, even on those rare occasions when something approaching a consensus emerged, I could detect no subsequent effect on policy.[10]

According to the theory of bureaucracy, this is what, in fact, we should expect. Policymaking is an "art" which is heavily dependent on inside information and expertise. Consistent with the theory of bureaucracy, the Federal Reserve simply undercut and disregarded the knowledge that would constrain it. And indeed, in reply to a letter in 1969 from Friedman regarding Federal Reserve use of monetary aggregates as targets, Chairman William M. Martin replied that, in effect, it was not whether the Federal Reserve could control the money supply, it was, rather, whether such control was desirable.[11]

Friedman's view of Martin's reply and what he later learned of the affair is certainly consistent with our theory. He discovered that the whole episode was simply to immobilize him. Why indeed bother figuring out something which the Federal Reserve System already knew but simply would not put into practice.[12]

Again, as our theory suggests, it is the agency itself that is important and not individuals, distinguished though they may be. Thus in 1970, when Arthur Burns became chairman, Friedman writes, "Monetary growth was put first and money market conditions second. However, that change turned out to be pure lip service and was later de-emphasized."[13]

Congress passed Concurrent Resolution 133 in 1975, which expressed the sentiments of Congress that the Federal Reserve control monetary aggregates, and consult and report to Congress at regular intervals. This was a resolution strongly opposed by the Federal Reserve. When passed, the Federal Reserve pledged cooperation. Within two years, the Federal Reserve undermined the resolution.[14]

If Congress has not been able to bend the Federal Reserve to its will, a recent study suggests that past Presidents have been more successful. It is argued that since the Treasury-Federal Reserve accord of March 1951, American presidents have been, in fact, the principal political influence behind Federal Reserve policy. According to the evidence cited in the study, its policy was significantly changed in 1953, 1961, 1969, 1971, 1974 and 1977—all years in which the presidency changed. This is consistent with our theory, since risk avoidance would push the Federal Reserve to pay closer attention to presidential desires than to those of Congress. It is the president and his administration that can directly threaten its status as an agency. The president does have the power to name the chairman of the Federal Reserve Board and at least two other members of the board during each presidential term. There is, moreover, a close working relationship between the administration and the Federal Reserve Board.[15]

It is significant, for instance, that during the important monetary policy changes between 1950 and 1970, the same individual, William M. Martin, was chairman. The strong presidential influence under which the central bankers of the Federal Reserve operate is suggested by events during the tenure of President Johnson (1963–69). These are also the years when market participants began to realize that significant changes were occurring in the country's monetary system away from a constrained specie-like system to an unconstrained government fiat standard.

Additional confirmation of presidential influence on the Federal Reserve is provided by the Nixon Administration (1969–74), when Arthur Burns served as chairman. In 1972, when Nixon was running for re-election, the old M1 definition of the money supply grew at almost 8.5 percent during the last quarter of 1972 and the first quarter of 1973, or at better than 6 percent during the period 1969–74. This is indeed, up to that time, a postwar record growth in the money supply. President Nixon also removed the country's last links with gold in 1971. To this may be added the administration's futile attempts to hold down inflation by price and wage controls and guidelines while promoting an expansive monetary policy.

During the Ford and subsequent Carter administration, monetary policy registered an indifferent performance. Ford succeeded in slowing monetary growth during his tenure (August 1974 to December 1976) by holding to his priority to bring down inflation. Arthur Burns was chairman of the Federal Reserve during this period.

At first, Carter considered inflation a non-monetary phenomenon and promoted monetary growth with the idea of lowering interest rates and encouraging investment. Arthur Burns continued to serve as Federal Reserve chairman until March 1978, when Carter appointed G. William Miller to the position. In November 1978 President Carter changed priorities from stimulating the economy to fighting inflation that had spurted into double digits. From the previous high of over 8.5 percent rate of growth in the old M1 reached by October 1978, the money supply growth was slowed by March 1979. Thereafter it again took off with M1B growing at a 13 percent annual rate between March and October of 1979.

Paul Volcker became Chairman of the Federal Reserve in August 1979. On October 6, 1979, he announced that the Federal Reserve would henceforth concentrate directly on controlling the money supply and de-emphasize interest rates as targets. I have discussed elsewhere the performance of American monetary policy since 1979.[16] The study draws attention to President Reagan's comments suggesting that it might be a good idea to put the Federal Reserve under Treasury supervision. This may be a harbinger of policy changes.

We should also expect that an agency such as the Federal Reserve, in our example, would push its own version of "history." Such activities can range from outright concealment of information that might be unfavorable to it or helpful to its critics, to pushing a general framework within which agency activities are interpreted so as to minimize the danger that it will be accused of making serious agency error.

On this score, it is interesting that the Federal Reserve undertook an extensive examination of its experience with monetary aggregates. In a massive two-volume study, the conclusion reached is that "the basic operating procedure represents a sound approach to attaining long-run objectives set for monetary standards."[17]

Quite a few observers will agree with Friedman when he writes, "I believe that the fundamental explanation for the persistence and importance of bureaucratic inertia in the Federal Reserve System is the absence of a bottom line."[18] In short, the Federal Reserve operates in a manner consistent with our theory of bureaucracy.

It would thus appear that in the U.S. at least direct congressional influence on monetary policy is quite limited. Apparently, congressmen see little payoff in investing the considerable time and effort necessary to study monetary policy to make sensible recommendations to the monetary authorities. A congressman is more likely to focus on spending proposals that directly serve his constituents. Effects of monetary policy are more indirect and pervasive by comparison to direct spending measures.

A test devised by Professor T. Havrilesky yields results consistent with those discussed earlier by Robert Weintraub that in the U.S. the central monetary authorities respond to signals from the White House. Havrilesky's results suggest a close relation between monetary policy views of Treasury officials and unnamed "high officials" and what later happened to the money supply.[19]

Havrilesky's results are obtained by the use of an index of monetary policy "Signals from the Administration to the Federal Reserve (SAFER)" which he constructs from the weekly sum of every article in *The Wall Street Journal* from September 1, 1979 to December 31, 1984, in which the administration officials expressed a desire for an easier or tighter monetary policy. A call for an easier policy was rated plus 1 and a request for a tighter policy was rated minus 1. He then checked to see what effect, if any, the call had on the money supply later.

His results also suggest that the Federal Reserve is fully aware of the presidential popularity polls. In periods when the president enjoyed a high public rating, the administration appeared to have even greater influence on the Federal Reserve.

On the basis of such results President Reagan would appear to have had significant influence on the Federal Reserve. Reagan is arguably, in his second term and prior to the Iran-Contra Affair, the strongest president since Dwight D. Eisenhower.[20] Republican polls claim an approval rating up to 74 percent into his second term.

A New York Times/CBS poll put his approval at 68 percent, including 56 percent of black respondents. Even the more modest figure of 63 percent approval in the December 1985 Gallup sampling is the best ever for a president five years in office; at that stage in his presidency even Eisenhower managed only 58 percent. Most remarkable of all, Reagan is the only president since the advent of modern polling to show ratings on a rising trend at the five-year mark. His ratings are not based on an inaugural honeymoon or status as a war hero; they are based on his conduct of the office.

The results reported on by Havrilesky are but one of a growing body of studies on the vote-maximizing behavior of politicians and concomitant politically induced cycles in such key variables as unemployment, inflation and real disposable income or in policies such as government purchases, transfer payments, taxes and monetary growth.[21] Allen (1986) reports that the Federal Reserve not only accommodates Treasury borrowing regardless of the electoral process, but also provides extra accommodation prior to presidential and congressional elections. Weintraub (1978) and Tufte (1980) suggest that politically induced cycles exist because monetary growth accelerates two years prior to a presidential election and decelerates the two years following an election. The relationship apparently holds for all elections except for the Eisenhower years. Wooley (1980) on the other hand finds no relationship between changes in the monetary base and the length of time prior to an election. An electoral cycle in the money supply is reported by Ahmad (1983) and by Schneider and Frey (1983). Golden and Poterba (1980), on the other hand, find an insignificant relationship between the electoral cycle and the real money supply function. Beck (1982) reports that when the federal funds rate is used in a reaction function, the results do not support the existence of a politically induced cycle in monetary policy before the 1972 election. Cowart (1978), on the other hand, finds that there is indeed political party influence upon central bank policy in several European countries.

Cowart's results are certainly consistent with the limited degree of "independence" possessed by central banks and reported on in Macesich and Tsai (1982).[22] Such independence depends on (1) the method of appointment of governors; (2) the length of time that they serve; (3) whether they have legislated objectives clear enough to be a barrier to government intervention; and (4) whether their constitutions provide the bank or the government with the final authority for monetary policy. In practice, central banks may have rather less, or rather more, freedom than their charters suggest. This is likely to depend on tradition as well as on the personalities involved.

Only the German Bundesbank has final authority for monetary policy. The governor, moreover, is not directly appointed by the government. The National Bank of Yugoslavia is nominally an independent federal institution, established by federal law. The bank is managed by the governor, who is appointed by the Federal Assembly on the recommendation of the Federal Executive Council. He is responsible to both of these institutions for the implementation of bank operations and targets. The Federal Assembly and the Federal Executive Council decide monetary policy targets, and the National Bank is responsible only for their implementation. Nonetheless, in policy formulation, the National Bank plays a significant, if not dominant role, in monetary policy, thanks to ready acceptance of its proposals by policy-makers.

The central bank of the Netherlands has a clearly defined objective of price stability built into its constitution. On no other score could it be considered independent. In fact, the world's two oldest central banks, Riksbank of Sweden (1668) and the bank of England (1694) are clearly subservient to their governments in the formation of monetary policy. On occasion it is pointed out that in the United States and Germany, control of the central bank rests with a board composed of the heads of the several regional banks, thereby allowing for greater "independence" from the central bank.

In fact, some Federal Reserve officials are careful to stress that the central bank is independent within the government, not independent of it.[23] The Federal Reserve chairman and the other members of the Reserve Board are appointees of the president. This has prompted some chairmen of the Federal Reserve, including former Chairman Paul Volcker, to support the idea that the chairman should resign about a year after a president takes office, giving the president a chance to name his own chairman.

Whether such an arrangement would promote a clearly defined policy of rules that would remove the Federal Reserve from the political quagmire in which it finds itself stuck while in pursuit of illusory goals is open for discussion. Along with other central banks, the Federal Reserve finds itself in the uncomfortable position where monetary and fiscal policies meet. They must meet the requirements of their governments. This means ensuring that the government is able to function smoothly in meeting its financial obligations. In many countries, government borrowing in the 1970s and 1980s has resulted in regular deficits, and debt has risen as a proportion of gross national product.

Concern with inflation calls attention to the growth in the money supply. Governments have reacted by setting formal targets for monetary growth. Since central banks must now try to achieve monetary targets while at the same time ostensibly financing much larger public sector borrowing, their job is made all the more difficult. Their lack of enthusiasm in embracing monetarism is understandable. Such an embrace would impose severe constraints on the exercise of discretionary monetary authority.

The absence of a bottom line in the form of a clearly defined policy of rules permits the Federal Reserve to simply guess what the administration wants. Despite what the chairman of the Federal Reserve tells Congress, the public will have to guess what the Federal Reserve will actually do. Such a state of affairs has prompted many economists and most notably Milton Friedman to observe that sooner or later we shall have a major financial crisis that will make possible a major monetary reform—one that will provide an anchor for the long-term price level.

NOTES

1. Milton Friedman, "The Role of Monetary Policy" in *The Optimum Quantity of Money and Other Essays*, Milton Friedman, ed. (Chicago: Aldine, 1969): p. 99. See also George Macesich, *Monetarism: Theory and Policy* (New York: Praeger Publishers, 1983), as well as the bibliography cited in these studies. Friedman writes, "Personally, I do not like the term monetarism. I would prefer to talk simply about the quantity theory of money, but we can't avoid usage that custom imposes on us" in "Monetary Policy: Theory and Practice," *Journal of Money, Credit and Banking* (February 1982): p. 101.

2. John M. Culbertson, *Macroeconomic Theory and Stabilization Policy* (New York: McGraw-Hill Book Company, 1968): p. 545.

3. See Assar Lindbeck, "Stabilization Policy with Endogenous Politicians" (Richard T. Ely Lecture), *The American Economic Review* (May 1976): 1–19.

4. George Macesich, *Monetarism: Theory and Policy*: pp. 43–60.

5. See George Macesich and Charles T. Stewart, Jr., "Recent Department of Labor Studies of Minimum Wage Effects," *Southern Economic Journal* (April 1960); Marshall R. Colberg, "Minimum Wage Effects on Florida Economic Development," *Journal of Law and Economics* (October 1960); John M. Peterson, "Recent Needs in Minimum Wage Theory," *Southern Economic Journal* (July 1962); Yale Brozen, "Minimum Wages and Household Workers," *Journal of Law and Economics* (October 1962); and L. G. Reynolds, "Wages and Employment in the Labor-Surplus Economy," *American Economic Review* (March 1965).

6. Macesich and Stewart, "Recent Department of Labor Studies": pp. 288ff.

7. George Macesich, "Are Wage Differentials Resilient? An Empirical Test," *Southern Economic Journal* (April 1961).

8. For a discussion on these issues see J. M. Culbertson, *Macroeconomic Theory and Stabilization Policy* (New York: McGraw-Hill Book

Company, 1968): pp. 410–11. See also, A. Downs, *Inside Bureaucracy* (Boston: Little Brown, 1967); H. G. Johnson, "Problems of Efficiency in Monetary Management, *Journal of Political Economy* (October 1968): pp. 971–90; Keith Hebeson and John F. Chant, "Bureaucratic Theory and the Choice of Central Bank Goals: The Case of the Bank of Canada," *Journal of Money, Credit and Banking* (May 1973): pp. 637–55; P. Selznik, "Foundations of the Theory of Organizations," *American Sociological Review* 13 (1948), reprinted as F. E. Emery, ed. *Systems Thinking* (Hammondsworth: Penguin Books, 1969); O. F. Williamson, *The Economics of Discretionary Behavior: Managerial Objectives in a Theory of the Firm* (Chicago: Markham Publishing Company, 1964); Albert Breton and Ronald Wintrobe, *The Logic of Bureaucratic Conduct* (Cambridge: Cambridge University Press, 1982).

9. Friedman, Milton, "Monetary Policy: Theory and Practice," *Journal of Money, Credit and Banking*, (February 1982): p. 98.

10. Ibid.

11. Ibid., p. 106.

12. Ibid.

13. Ibid.

14. See James L. Pierce, "The Myth of Congressional Supervision of Monetary Policy," *Journal of Monetary Economics* (April 1978), reprinted in Thomas M. Havrilesky and John T. Boorman, eds. *Current Issues in Monetary Theory and Policy*, 2nd edition (Arlington Heights, IL.: AHM Publishing Company, 1980): p. 482.

15. Robert E. Weintraub, "Congressional Supervision of Monetary Policy," *Journal of Monetary Economics* (April 1978): pp. 341–62. See also, Robert D. Auerbach, *Money, Banking and Financial Markets* (New York: Macmillan Company, 1982): pp. 362ff.

16. See George Macesich, *The Politics of Monetarism: Its Historical and Institutional Development* (Totowa, NJ: Rowman and Allanheld, 1984): Chapter 6.

17. *New Monetary Control Procedures*, Federal Reserve Staff Study, Vols. 1 and 2 (Washington, D.C. Board of Governors of the Federal Reserve System, February 1982).

18. Milton Friedman, "Monetary Policy: Theory and Practice": p. 124.

19. Lindley H. Clark, Jr., "Wigwagging from the White House to the Fed," *The Wall Street Journal* (January 28, 1986): p. 31.

20. Robert L. Bartley, "Reagan in Command at a Crucible," *The Wall Street Journal* (January 28, 1986).

21. Stuart D. Allen, "The Federal Reserve and the Electoral Cycle," *Journal of Money, Credit and Banking* (February 1986): pp. 88–94; B. S. Frey and F. Schneider, "An Empirical Study of Politico-Economic In-

teraction in the U.S.: A Reply," *Review of Economics and Statistics* (February 1983): pp. 178–82; K. U. Ahmad, "An Empirical Study of Politico-Economic Interaction in the U.S.: A Comment," *Review of Economics and Statistics* (February 1983): pp. 173–78; N. Beck, "Presidential Influence on the Federal Reserve in the 1970's," *American Journal of Political Science* (August 1982): pp. 415–45; M. D. Levy, "Factors Affecting Monetary Policy in an Era of Inflation," *Journal of Monetary Economics* (November 1981): pp. 351–74; M. Paldam, "A Preliminary Survey of Theories and Findings on Vote Popularity Functions," *European Journal of Political Research* 9 (1981): pp. 181–99; M. Paldam, "An Essay on the Rationality of Economic Policy: The Test-Case of the Electional Cycle," *Public Choice* 37 (1981): pp. 287–305; J. Wooley, "The Federal Reserve System and the Political Economy of Monetary Policy," (Ph.D. dissertation, University of Wisconsin, 1980); D. G. Golden and J. M. Poterba, "The Price of Popularity: The Political Business Cycle Reexamined," *American Journal of Political Science* (November 1980): pp. 698–714; B. S. Frey, "Politico-Economic Models and Choice," *Journal of Public Economics* (April 1978): pp. 203–20; B. S. Frey and F. Schneider, "An Empirical Study of Politico-Economic Interaction in the U.S.," *Review of Economics and Statistics* (May 1978): pp. 174–83; B. S. Frey and F. Schneider, "Central Bank Behavior: A Positive Empirical Analysis," *Journal of Monetary Economics* (May 1981): pp. 291–315; E. R. Tufte, *Political Control of the Economy* (Princeton: Princeton University Press, 1978); B. T. McCallum, "The Political Business Cycle: An Empirical Test," *Southern Economic Journal* (January 1978): pp. 169–90; A. T. Cowart, "The Economic Policies of European Governments, Part I: Monetary Policy," *British Journal of Political Science* (July 1978): pp. 285–311; R. J. Gordon, "The Demand for and Supply of Inflation," *Journal of Law and Economics* (December 1975): pp. 807–36; See George Macesich and H. Tsai, *Money in Economic Systems* (New York: Praeger Publishers, 1982).

22. George Macesich on Federal Reserve independence and ownership, "Stock and the Federal Reserve System," U.S. Congress, House, Subcommittee on Domestic Finance of the Committee on Banking and Currency, *Compendium on Monetary Policy Guidelines and Federal Reserve Structure*, 90th Congress, 2nd Session (Washington, DC: U.S. Government Printing Office, December 1968) and Macesich, "Central Banking, Monetary Policy and Economic Activity": pp. 437–54.

23. *The Wall Street Journal* (February 18, 1986): p. 33.

Chapter 2

Struggle for Monetary Supremacy: An American Experience

"BANK WAR": 1833–34

The early assertion of an important role for the American president in monetary affairs is underscored in the struggle for monetary supremacy between the partisans of the Second Bank of the United States and the federal government and especially the collision between the Bank's president, Nicholas Biddle, and President Andrew Jackson. The episode is also a good illustration of implicit presidential support for a rules based monetary policy in the form of a specie standard and, in effect, an anchor for the general level of prices. It is useful to examine this experience for the insights it provides for contemporary events.

Briefly, the partisans of the Second Bank attributed the economic and monetary turmoil during the 1830s in the United States to the elimination by the federal government of the Second Bank as a depository for federal funds and as a national institution.[1] In effect, the partisans of the Second Bank argue that the federal government by its policies had at first promoted an autonomous increase in the country's money supply and later reversed itself and promoted an autonomous decrease in the money supply. The federal government did, in fact, at first encourage the new depository banks into which federal government deposits were placed along with other banks to expand their operations. It is also true that the federal government shortly thereafter repudiated the new depository banks and the banking system in general by its issue of the Specie Circular (1836). Given that the United States was on the international specie standard, and at the time recipient of substantial capital imports and subsequent cessation of such imports, the fact that banks expanded and later contracted their numbers, notes, and deposits was only partly the form taken by the expansion and subsequent contraction that would have occurred one way or another.

Arithmetic aside, the economic significance of the internal American monetary turmoil is that it was an important source of the country's short-term monetary uncertainty and in this way affected the links between external and internal forces. For the purposes at hand, consider briefly the Second Bank of the United States following 1833, hard currency policy (Specie Circular) of the federal government and the Deposit Act of 1836, the first and second suspensions, and the Independent Treasury proposals.

According to contemporaries and more recent students, the Second Bank had three distinctive methods with which to affect "favorably" or, for that matter, "unfavorably" the country's money supply: it was the depository of federal funds; it exercised "proper restraint" in its dealings as a private bank. By skillfully employing these methods, it is held, the Bank was able to wield control over state banks and through them ultimately over the money supply. The process of control was simplicity itself: The Bank merely presented the bank notes of the state banks for payment when they fell into its hands. Contemporaries emphasized that the stability of the country's currency depended almost exclusively on this measure.[2]

As to the effects of these operations, evidence is presented that state bank notes everywhere prior to 1834 had been either driven out of circulation or made redeemable in specie.[3] However, all of this is consistent with the Second Bank having little or no effect on the money supply. That is to say, the views of contemporaries, as well as those of more recent students, are subject to several criticisms. In the first instance, the possession of numerous branches might simply have resulted in the circulation of the notes of the Second Bank instead of the notes of state banks. This does not mean that the availability of a relatively uniform currency might not have been economically advantageous. It does mean, however, that the possession of numerous branches is consistent with little or no effect on the total money supply. In the second instance, the exercise of "proper restraint" in its dealings as a private bank is asserted as a method for keeping state banks in debt to the

Second Bank. By keeping state banks in debt, it is said, the Second Bank restricted their operations with a threat of a call for specie. However, the serious employment of this method would almost certainly have resulted in making the Second Bank a smaller institution. Indeed, if it made no loans and issued no notes it would simply go out of business. The real method of control over state banks seems to have stemmed from the Bank's position as a depository for federal funds.[4] In its position as a federal depository, state banks in all payments to the government had to satisfy the Bank of the United States that their notes were equivalent to specie before the government would receive them, and if the government refused them, a source of extensive circulation was closed. In this manner, the Bank could face a state bank with the alternative of operating on a specie paying basis or having its business severely restricted and the credit of its notes destroyed. However, in order to see what the real effects of the Bank's actions were on the money supply, one must see what its effect was on international economic movements. The reason for this becomes obvious when it is recalled that the United States was on the international specie standard.

In its effects on international economic movements, and thus on the money supply, the operations of the Second Bank seem to merit particular attention only on two occasions for the purpose of this study. The first is during the so-called "Bank War" in 1833–34. The second is following the suspension of specie payments in 1837.

The "Bank War" is particularly interesting to this study. The actions of the federal government to deprive the Bank of federal deposits as well as its federal charter and the effort of the Bank to dissuade the government from this course of action have seldom been paralleled in monetary history. Indeed, in many respects the course of events may be viewed as an early forerunner to the contests between central bankers and central governments in more recent history.

With the appointment of new depository banks in 1833, the Second Bank lost its profitable monopoly and the "Bank War" began in earnest.[5] The government deposits were not withdrawn at once. The deposits were allowed to run down in the normal course of government disbursements.[6] The entire matter of de-

Table 2.1
Second Bank of the United States, Loans and Discounts ($ thousands)

Date	Specie	Total Loans	Discounts	Bills of Exchange
August 1, 1833......	$10,023	$64,100	$43,200	$20,900
October 1, 1833.....	N.A.	60,000	42,200	17,800
January 1, 1834.....	10,040	54,900	38,600	16,300
September 30, 1834..	15,510	47,000	34,800	12,100

Source: Senate Document 128, 25th Cong., 2d Sess., : 208-211.

posits, however, soon fell into the political arena. Two secretaries of the treasury, Louis McLane and William Duane, were dropped by President Jackson before a pliable secretary was obtained in the person of Roger B. Taney to implement the government's policy.

The Second Bank, in turn, began to curtail its operations in August 1833 with a view first to strengthening its position and second to forcing the return of government deposits and its rechartering as a national institution. Table 2.1 presents evidence on the severity of the Second Bank's contraction of loans and discounts. For this study, the accumulation of specie by the Second Bank is even more significant. The sum was a little over ten million dollars at the beginning of August 1833. It was fifteen and one-half million dollars at the end of September 1834. It had never before reached within four million dollars of that amount.

The accumulation of specie by the Second Bank is highly relevant to international economic movements and thus to the money supply. In effect, the accumulation of specie was equivalent to a capital export. This means that the United States had to have a favorable balance, or less unfavorable one, in foreign trade sufficient to provide this specie. This in turn could be produced only by a lower price level in the United States relative to external prices. The evidence seems consistent with this explanation. Thus, there is a sharp drop in the United States commodity import surplus from 1833 to 1834 and an increase in specie imports along with a high ratio of import to export prices in the same period.

It was pointed out that the United States was receiving capital imports in this period. It would seem that the above two positions are inconsistent; they are not. It simply means that a larger specie supply was required to activate the international adjustment mechanism of the specie standard. By accumulating specie the Second Bank, in effect, offset part of the capital inflow causing the money supply to decline, or rise relatively less than would otherwise have been the case.

As one would expect, the Second Bank's contraction threw the country into an economic panic. Evidence suggests that the maneuvers of the Second Bank were politically inspired and completely neglected events in other sectors of the economy. For example, as early as November, 1833, Biddle had privately admitted that the Second Bank was "entirely beyond the reach of any mischief from the Treasury."[7]

Relief committees traveled from one contestant to another without obtaining the desired results.[8] Indeed, the partisans of the Second Bank felt that the relief committees were rendering the Bank a valuable service by impressing the federal government with the Bank's importance.[9] The panic was, however, short-lived and for the remainder of 1834, the economy was on the upswing.

As a result of the so-called "Bank War," the Second Bank of the United States was stripped of its monopoly powers. Quantitatively, the importance of the Second Bank decreased progressively over the period of this study. For example, as illustrated in Table 2.2, the ratio of loans and discounts of the Bank to total

Table 2.2
Second Bank of the United States: Loans and Discounts, Due to and from State Banks, 1831–40 (January) ($ thousands)

Year	Loans and Discount	Ratio of U.S.B. Loans and Discounts to Total Loans and Discounts of All Banks	Ratio of U.S.B. Specie to Total Specie of All Banks	Due to State Banks	Due From State Banks	Ratio Due To Due From
1831	$44,032	...	...	$ 735	$1,495	.49
1832	66,294	...	...	1,951	6,117	.32
1833	61,696	...	...	2,092	6,611	.32
1834	54,911	.17	.38	1,522	5,042	.30
1835	51,809	.14	.36	3,199	6,206	.50
1836	59,232	.13	.21	2,661	5,824	.46
1837	57,394	.11	.07	2,285	3,492	.65
1838	45,257	.09	.11	4,957	4,524	1.09
1839	41,619	.08	.09	3,062	7,625	.40
1840	36,840	.08	.04	4,155	8,853	.47

Source: Comptroller of Currency Report for 1876.

loans and discounts of all banks as well as the ratio of specie held by the Bank to total specie held by all banks declined unsteadily from 1834 to 1840. Furthermore, the Second Bank of the United States disclaimed any further "responsibility" for the conditions of the country's currency.[10]

In conclusion, the "Bank War" shows that on occasion political circumstances, independent of events in other sectors of the economy, can be important in affecting a country's money supply. Moreover, the "Bank War" is instructive for the light it sheds on the so-called "independence of a central bank." This central bank, albeit a primitive one, saw its policies fail and its existence threatened when these policies were such that they opposed the policies of the central government.

As mentioned earlier, the other period of interest in the Second Bank is that following the suspension of specie payments in 1837. This will be discussed subsequently along with the period of suspension.

THE HARD CURRENCY POLICY AND DEPOSIT ACT OF 1836

With the destruction of the Second Bank as a source of power, the federal government undertook the first of a series of reforms the objective of which was to give the country a "hard currency."

The first of these reforms occurred on June 24, 1834, with the passage of legislation changing the mint ratio from 15 to 1 to 16 to 1.[11] This legislation in effect over-valued gold vis-à-vis silver. In pressing for the adoption of the new mint ratio, the government's argument was that the new mint ratio would change the supply conditions of gold in the United States. At the same time the government argued that the increased supply of gold currency would displace bank currency. As the Washington *Globe* said with some party rancor:

> The Bank Party, even in the Senate, has been obliged to vote for the measure of the Administration deemed essential to carry out its policy . . . they have been forced to vote for the Gold Bill, which is a measure of deadly hostility to the interests of the Bank, will supersede its notes, and is a harbinger of a *real* sound currency. The people understand the

> policy of the Administration and . . . see that it would give them Gold instead of paper. The great Bank attorney, Mr. Clay . . . voted against the Bill . . . but carried only six Bank Senators with him . . . they voted for the Bill . . . dared not tell the people, "*We will deny you gold, and will force you to depend . . . on the notes of the mammoth Bank.*" Thus were they forced to minister to the triumph of the Administration.[12]

Discussion prior to the adoption of the ratio of 16 to 1 favored a single standard: silver. The reasons given for this preference were that contracts for many years had been based on the silver dollar and that no exact adjustment of the bimetallic ratio could be maintained with any degree of permanence. Moreover, it was felt that the country could not get along without silver but could without gold by the use of sound bank currency. Secretary of the Treasury Ingham on May 4, 1830, in response to a resolution of the Senate, December 20, 1828, suggested that since it was desirable under his plan to have gold at a slight premium, the desirable coinage ratio would be 15.625 to 1. In May 1834 the banks of New York, under the lead of Albert Gallatin, then president of one of them, sent a memorandum to Congress asking for the enactment of a law to coin gold at the rate of 23.76 grains of pure and 25.92 grains of standard metal to the dollar. This would have continued the fineness of coin at .916–2/3 (or 11/12) and since the silver dollar remained unchanged, would have resulted in a ratio 15.625 to 1. They also asked that silver of the Latin American States and five franc pieces of France be made legal tender as well as Spanish dollars at their mint values. The silver coins of these countries had in fact become the chief elements in the specie circulation of the United States. Representative C.P. White of New York, a key member of the House Committee studying gold and silver, recommended the adoption of 15.625 to 1 and .900 as standard fineness. But one week before the passage of the act, Representative White reversed himself and reported a bill which favored a gold rather than a silver standard by fixing a ratio of about 16 to 1. Consequently, the new mint ratio made the United States a competitor for the world's stock of gold.[13]

The change in the mint ratio was accompanied by a concentrated effort by federal and state governments to suppress the issue of small denomination notes. Small denomination bank notes had, for the most part, the dubious distinction of possessing for many years the highest rates of depreciation in terms of specie. Although as early as 1832, it was recommended that bank notes of ten dollars and under be prohibited,[14] the measure was finally passed in 1835. On April 6, 1835, the Treasury notified collecting and receiving agents of public revenue that after November 30, 1835, they were not to receive in payment bank notes of any denomination less than five dollars.[15] Moreover, on March 3, 1836, the denomination of bank notes not receivable in payment to the government was increased, effective July 4, 1836, to ten dollars.[16] To re-enforce the measures against small denomination bank notes, it was provided that no bank would be appointed by the federal government as a depository which issued notes in denominations of less than ten dollars.[17] Unfortunately, it is difficult to know how successful these measures were, since there is no information available on the quantity of these notes outstanding.

The federal government was not satisfied, however, with the course of monetary affairs. There was particular dissatisfaction with the southern and western sections of the United States. In this period these sections of the country were literally doing a "land-office" business.[18] It was, however, a business in which the federal government felt that it and small purchasers were, as a matter of course, being victimized. In order to protect itself as well as the smaller purchasers, the government implemented the third of its series of reforms to achieve a "hard currency." On July 11, 1836, the Treasury Department issued what is termed the "Specie Circular." This circular was an order instructing agents for the sale of public lands to take in payment only specie and no longer receive the notes issued by banks. As the Secretary of the Treasury put it:

> In consequence of complaints which have been made of frauds, speculations, monopolies, in the purchase of public lands, and the aid which is said to be given to effect these objects by excessive bank credits, and dangerous if not partial facilities through bank drafts and bank deposites [*sic*], and the general evil influence likely to result to the public interests, and especially the safety of the great amount of money in the Treasury and the sound condition of the country, from further exchange of the national domain in this manner, and chiefly for bank credits and paper money, the President . . . has given directions, that you are hereby in-

structed after the 15th day of August next, to receive in payment of the public lands nothing except what is directed by the existing laws, viz: gold and silver.[19]

Almost simultaneously Congress authorized that the surplus in the Treasury above five million dollars be distributed among the states in proportion to their population. The distribution was to be made in quarterly installments beginning January 1, 1837. This was the Deposit Act or "distribution of the surplus revenue." At the time of passage of this bill the surplus in the Treasury amounted to approximately forty-one million dollars.[20]

Although a good case can be made for treating the Specie Circular and Deposit Act separately, the limitations of data make it difficult to differentiate their separate effects on the money supply. Consequently, the remainder of this section will treat them as a single disturbance.

As expected the effect of the Specie Circular and Deposit Act was to produce a substantial internal shift in the "specie ballast" affecting bank reserves and ultimately the money supply. In this context it is interesting to quote at length Biddle's views on these two disturbances:

The combination of these two measures (Specie Circular and Deposit Act) produced a double result—first, to require banks generally to increase their specie, and next to give them the means for doing it by drafts on the deposit banks. The commercial community was taken by surprise. The interior banks making no loans and converting their Atlantic funds into specie, the debtors in the interior could make no remittances to the merchants in the Atlantic cities, who were thus thrown for support on the banks of those cities, at a moment when they were unable to afford relief on account of the very abstraction of their specie to the West. The creditor States, not only receive no money, but their money is carried away by debtor States, who in turn can not use it either to pay old engagements or to contract new. By this unnatural process the specie of New York and other commercial cities is piled up in the Western States—not Treasury—and while the West cannot use it—the East is suffering from the want of it. The result is that the commercial intercourse between the West and Atlantic is wholly suspended, and the few operations which are made are burdened with most extravagant expenses . . . while Europe is alarmed and the bank of England itself uneasy at the quantity of specie we possess

> . . . we are suffering . . . the whole ballast of the currency is shifted from one side of the vessel to the other.[21]

Biddle's views of the effects of the Specie Circular coupled with the effects of the Deposit Act on internal monetary conditions were apparently shared by other contemporaries. As *Hazard,* a contemporary reviewer of economic affairs, reports:

> Millions upon millions of coins were *in transitu* in every direction and consequently withdrawn from useful employment. Specie was going up and down the same river, to and from the South and North, East and West at the same time; millions were withdrawn from their usual and natural channels of trade and forced against the current of trade in literal fulfillment of the distribution law (Deposit Act), to points where public money had previously never been collected or expended except to a limited extent.[22]

If we take the views of contemporaries seriously, we should expect to observe the following: first, that the West and Southwest gained specie at the expense of the East; second, that bank discounts and loans in both the West and Southwest as well as the East declined or at least leveled off; third, that other parts of the country received government deposits at the expense of the principal eastern, western, and southwestern states.[23]

The evidence available for the country as a whole on an annual basis does suggest that from 1836 to 1837 the West and Southwest gained specie at the expense of the East.[24] Except for two states, one western (Indiana) and one eastern (Pennsylvania), evidence for this period on a less than annual basis is almost unobtainable. The discounts of the State Bank of Indiana indicate that following a rapid increase in 1835, they leveled off at 2.7 million dollars between the middle and the end of the year 1836, while simultaneously circulation declined and specie increased.[25] Pennsylvania information indicates that following the rapid expansion in 1834–36, discounts and notes leveled off in mid-1836 while specie thereafter slightly increased.[26]

Throughout 1836, the Treasury continued to adjust its balances between depository banks and states in preparation for the January 1 transfer to the states. These operations by the Treasury suggest a reason for the rapid rise in commercial paper rates in New York in mid-1836. In August the rate increased rapidly to 18 percent on "first class bankable paper"; by the end of the year the rate had advanced to 30 percent. Following the distribution of the first transfer, money rates declined slightly. Almost immediately, however, the banks prepared for the second transfer to take place in April. Money market rates again advanced to 30 percent. Within four months, from January to April, the New York depository banks lost over six million dollars.

As the second transfer was going to the states, and the banks in turn were preparing for the third transfer, the New York banks on May 10, 1837, suspended specie payments.[27] With the spread of suspension, the notes of the various banks varied in their rates of depreciation. This state of affairs prompted the secretary of the treasury, in issuing the order for the July transfer, to inform the State authorities that they were not required to accept the depreciated currency but could return the transfer to the secretary. The secretary would in turn submit the matter to Congress. No instance has been found where a state did this.[28] Apparently, the states preferred to take a depreciated currency rather than to wait.

The first three transfers came mainly from the eastern seaboard states. The deposits in the southern and western banks that had failed were not available. In October 1837, there still remained nine million dollars on deposit in the West and Southwest—a sum equal to the fourth transfer.

Consequently, the fourth transfer due in October was cancelled. Indeed, there was no surplus to transfer. By October 1837, the Treasury obtained authority to issue one-year notes in order to meet current expenses.

Although the Deposit Act of 1836 was considered by the government as a measure requiring the temporary deposit of government funds in the various states, the states interpreted the measure as a straightforward distribution of funds. For example, Virginia in 1883 brought suit to the Supreme Court for its share of the fourth transfer.[29]

Before we turn in more detail to the period of suspension of specie payments in 1837, let us briefly recapitulate the internal disturbances discussed above. In effect, the federal government was seeking to maintain the specie standard. But the ability of the government to do so, as expressed in the Specie Circular and

Deposit Act, was uncertain. The approximate origin of the increase in distrust in the ability of the government to maintain the specie standard was probably the operation of the Deposit Act itself. Public misgivings about the maintenance of the specie standard soon became intensified when it became clear that not all of the government's depository banks would be able to meet the provisions of the Deposit Act. The attempts by depository banks in particular and by all banks in general to increase their specie reserve coupled with the firm refusal of the government to repeal the Specie Circular merely increased the suspicion and made desirable an increase in the public's specie-money ratio.

FIRST AND SECOND SUSPENSIONS AND THE INDEPENDENT TREASURY PROPOSALS

The serious difficulties of the period 1836–37 seem to have their origin in the combination of two forces. In the first place external prices fell sharply. This alone would have required a decline in internal prices in the United States. In the second place, this period saw the peak of agitation and victory by the political forces in favor of a "hard currency." The victory was expressed by the passage of the Specie Circular and Deposit Act. The effect was to create a lack of confidence both at home and abroad in the maintenance of the specie standard and to lead to a "flight" from the dollar.[30] The financing of this adverse capital movement put still further pressure on internal prices. Rather than to take the adjustments required by the specie standard, the United States suspended specie payments in the spring of 1837.

When the banks of New York suspended specie payments in May 1837, banks in other parts of the country quickly followed the example of those in New York. Although various states legally sanctioned the suspension, it was viewed as a temporary expedient. The suspension of specie payments meant in principle the inversion of the role of the stock of money. Internal monetary changes affected the price level and threw out the exchange rate. Internal prices, at first, increased following suspension and then decreased as a prelude to resumption. Specie went to a premium and exchange in London, which was tantamount to command over specie, inevitably moved in the same direction and to the same degree.

Suspension brought an end to the many business failures. The pressure on the money market was relieved and by July rates stood at 6 percent for "first class bankable paper" in New York. If suspension brought relief, it also introduced a dual monetary system—specie and bank money not interchangeable at a fixed rate. As noted above, the specie premium was equivalent to depreciation of the bank dollar in terms of specie or foreign exchange and since the suspension was not expected to last, gave an incentive to convert foreign balances into dollars.[31]

The suspension, by creating a dual monetary system, also reduced the usefulness of bank money. This made the given nominal stock of money equivalent to a smaller stock with free interchangeability. Moreover, insofar as the dual monetary system needed more of both bank money and specie, it led the public to desire to increase its ratio of specie to bank money.

Imports of specie were supplemented by issues of Treasury notes to meet current governmental expenditures in the latter part of 1837.[32] During the suspension, the want of small change was such as to induce various measures to meet its absence. One device was the issue of fractional bills for $1.25, $1.50, $1.75.[33] Another device, for a brief period, was the issue of spurious copper coin to supply the absence of cents.[34] Unfortunately, estimates for this period are not available either for the quantity of fractional bank notes outstanding or for the quantity of spurious coin outstanding.

Given that the suspension was not expected to last, it had implications for the required behavior of the money stock. But this required behavior had to be achieved by policy action; there were no "automatic" forces bringing it about. Consequently, the remainder of this section will examine briefly the operations of the two contestants for monetary supremacy: the Second Bank, now a Pennsylvania institution, and its policy which favored continued suspension; the federal government and its policy which favored immediate resumption.

Contemporaries report that it was in the late summer of 1837 when banks seriously started to contract their operations. The East contracted its operations the sharpest in the period 1837–38 followed by the West and lastly by the Southwest.[35] Between 1837 and 1838, loans and discounts in the East declined by 40 percent. From data available on a less than annual basis for two key states,

New York and Pennsylvania, the information indicates that during the period of suspension the severest contraction had taken place in New York.[36] The banks of New York from June 1837 to May 1838, contracted their loans and discounts by 23 percent; their notes by 20 percent, and their deposits by 23 percent; Pennsylvania banks contracted loans and discounts by 12 percent and notes and deposits by 10 percent. In the West, during the same period, the State Bank of Indiana contracted its loans and discounts by 25 percent, notes by 5 percent, and deposits by 16 percent. As was to be expected, pressure in a money market increase, rates advanced and reached 18 percent in March and April 1838.

The money supply contracted by 2 percent and the annual indexes of internal prices decreased by an average of 3 percent in the period from 1837–38. The subsequent resumption was made easier by an increase in external prices from 1837–38.

On May 10, 1838, the banks of New York resumed specie payments and were soon followed by others throughout the country.

As the banks of New York were preparing for resumption, Biddle was counselling the banks as well as the public that the credit system and the specie system were face to face and one or the other must fall.[37]

> The credit system of the United States and the exclusive metallic system are now fairly in the field, face to face with each other . . . If the banks resume and are able, by sacrificing the community, to continue for a few months it will be exclusively employed at the next election to show that the schemes of the executive are not as destructive as they will prove hereafter. But if they resume and are again compelled to suspend, the executive will rejoice in this new triumph, and they will fall in the midst of a universal outcry against their weakness.[38]

In effect, Biddle was stalling. He did not point out that the solvency of the Bank was tied up with the solvency of the debtor areas of the country.[39] Despite Biddle's efforts, the governor of Pennsylvania proclaimed August 13, 1838, as the date for resumption. Furthermore, Biddle's pretext for inconvertibility no longer existed: The Specie Circular was repealed on May 31.

Biddle interpreted the repeal of the Specie Circular as a victory for the "credit system":

Remember that whatever you may read to the contrary, the repeal of the Specie Circular and defeat of the Sub-Treasury are the results, exclusively of the course pursued by the Bank of the United States. If we had done as the New York banks, succumbed to the government when they did, it would have been a surrender.[40]

President Van Buren, of course, disagreed with Biddle's analysis. In his message to Congress in December 1838, Van Buren claimed that in addition to cancelling the fourth surplus, the government's refusal to employ as depositories or receive the notes of such banks as declined to redeem their notes in specie, coupled with the cooperation of a large part of the community, secured an early resumption.[41]

By 1839 the Bank was anything but a "prudent regulator of the country's currency." In fact, the Bank was becoming something of an embarrassment to the country.[42] Moreover, in 1839, the Bank began to conduct a rather interesting operation. It began to borrow in the New York money market on post-notes bearing interest at 18 to 24 percent. Simultaneously, with the exchange on London at a premium, it sold large quantities of drafts payable by its agent in London. Since both the post-notes and the drafts were in demand, the Bank acquired large amounts of specie and claims on New York banks. Its agent in London paid the drafts on London by shipment of specie purchased in New York with money realized by the sale of drafts and post-notes. With each transaction the Bank incurred a loss.[43] Contemporaries interpreted this operation as a desire of the Bank to supply itself with funds to support the cotton market. On the other hand, one of the Bank's officers at an inquiry following its subsequent suspension said:

Another crisis was anticipated, and it was feared that the banks generally would be obliged again to suspend. This was unhappily too soon to be realized, for the storm was then ready to burst; but instead of meeting its full force at once, it was deemed best to make it fall first upon the banks of New York.[44]

In other words, the "regulator of the currency" felt that another suspension was imminent, and to anticipate that event they acquired claims on New York banks by sales of post-notes and drafts on London with a view to forcing these banks to suspend immediately.

Needless to say, the effort failed and with confidence in it shaken, the Bank suspended on October 9. Thereafter its situation was hopeless,[45] for an inquiry after its suspension revealed that most of its assets were completely illiquid.

By October 14, news of the suspension reached Ohio. Shortly thereafter many banks in the West suspended and in this they were followed by others throughout the country. An effective resumption did not occur until March, 1842.

Let us turn briefly to the activities of the government. After the difficulties of 1837, the government felt that henceforth it should sever all connections with banks, collect its revenue in specie only and keep the same in its own possession until needed for disbursements. The recommendations of the government for an independent treasury were formulated into a bill and submitted to Congress where it was defeated. The opposition maintained that what was needed was a "uniform currency system which only a central bank could enforce." After a period of bitter political agitation the Independent Treasury became law on July 4, 1840.

The act provided for the collection, safekeeping, transfer, and disbursement of public money by the Treasury through treasurers and receivers-general, of whom a definite number were to be appointed for the purpose; public money was not to be loaned or deposited in banks, under severe penalties, except that when a large surplus was on hand, it might be especially deposited in banks designated by the secretary of the treasury, but could not be loaned by banks; the banks so used were to receive one-eighth percent commission; officers handling the funds were to be bonded; and vaults were to be built. The specie clause, an important feature which nearly killed the bill, was modified so as to have all public dues paid one-fourth in specie for the first year and an additional fourth each succeeding year until the whole was so payable.[46]

Although the Independent Treasury system by its design had potential power to affect the money supply, the system soon fell, once again, into the political arena. It was repealed on August 13, 1841, when the Whigs returned to power. Moreover, the effectiveness of the system was enfeebled by its lack of resources. It had inherited a few small accounts, remainders of the state bank depository system. By 1841, the total amount in the Treasury and deposit banks was only 1.7 million dollars.

After the repeal of the Independent Treasury, Treasury operations were made dependent upon the notes of specie paying banks. The growing government revenue, originating for the most part in customs receipts, was deposited in banks on terms similar to those of 1833.

In conclusion, the ebb and flow of the internal struggle during the period following suspension of specie payments in 1837 undoubtedly affected confidence in the monetary standard. In 1838, confidence in the monetary standard was temporarily restored when the Specie Circular was repealed and resumption of specie payments occurred. Confidence in the monetary standard also led the public to desire to decrease its ratio of specie to bank money. In effect, a temporary lull in the struggle occurred in 1838.

When the government submitted its proposals for the independent treasury in December 1838, it was a signal for the struggle to begin anew. The bitter struggle that followed aroused distrust of the maintenance of the specie standard and promoted a "flight" from the dollar. The financing of this adverse "flight" placed a downward pressure on prices. At the same time, external prices, as judged by Silberling's price index for Britain, declined in the third quarter of 1839. The decline in external prices was co-incident with a cessation of the heavy capital inflow of previous years. The combination of these two alone would have required a decline in internal prices.

In contrast with 1837, a general suspension in 1839 did not occur. This is attributed to a rapid internal decline of prices relative to the external prices which continued until 1843. This contraction had important effects on the banking structure of the United States, namely: the destruction of the Second Bank in 1841 and about a 25 percent decrease in the number of banks from 1840 to 1843. At the same time, the collapse of the banking system was caused partly by the manner in which an adjustment, forced by other circumstances, worked itself out. The price decline abroad, cessation of the large capital inflow of earlier years, repudiation of obligations, suspension of specie payments by some banks, and distrust both at home and abroad of the maintenance of the specie standard by the United States made a sizable decline in prices the only alternative to the abandonment of the specie standard and depreciation of the dollar relative to other currencies. Given the maintenance of the specie standard, such an adjustment was unavoidable; if it had not occurred partly through the banking collapse, it would have done so in some other way, such as an export of specie.

SUMMARY

In conclusion, the internal struggle for monetary supremacy was simultaneously a cause and a consequence of the economic difficulties in the period from 1834 to 1845. It was the cause of the economic difficulties for the reason that the internal struggle for monetary supremacy was a source of monetary uncertainty. But contrary to the views held by contemporaries and more recent students, the monetary damage done by the internal struggle and its concomitant uncertainty kept the money supply from rising as much as it otherwise would have in the period from 1834 to 1837 rather than that it produced too rapid a rise in the money supply. At the same time, the internal struggle for monetary supremacy was a consequence of the economic difficulties for the reason that the struggle was partly the form taken by adjustments forced by other circumstances, namely: external expansion and then contraction coupled with a capital inflow and then cessation of capital inflow.

NOTES

1. George Macesich, "Sources of Monetary Disturbance in the United States, 1834–1845," *Journal of Economic History* (September 1960): pp. 407–34.

2. H. R. 460, 22nd Cong., 1st Sess.: p. 363; H.O. Adams, ed. *Gallatin's Writings* (Philadelphia: Lippincott, 1879), III: p. 336.

3. H. R. 358, 21st Cong., 1st Sess.: p. 18 and *Niles' Weekly Register*, XXXIV: p. 154.

4. Total government deposits amounted to over $410 million during the entire period that the Second Bank held them. The importance of government deposits to the Second Bank may be seen from calculations made by Secretaries of the Treasury Taney and Catterall. Average government deposits estimated by Taney for every month from 1819 to 1833

amounted to over $6,717,253. Catterall computes the profits at six percent for the whole time that the Bank was a government depository. His computations indicated that the Bank was the gainer to the extent of $403,035.18 each year from 1818 to 1834—a total of $6,448,562.88. S.D. 16, 23rd Cong., 1st Sess.: pp. 4–5, and R. C. H. Catterall, *Second Bank of the United States* (Chicago: University of Chicago Press, 1903): p. 475.

5. "The whole question of peace or war lies in the matter of Deposites [*sic*]. If they are withdrawn, it is a declaration of war." *Biddle Papers* (Washington, D.C.: Manuscript Division, Library of Congress), Biddle to Webster, April 10, 1833.

6. Catterall, *Second Bank of the United States.*

7. *Biddle Papers*, Biddle to Verplanck, November 19, 1833.

8. Biddle persisted that "relief to be useful or permanent must come from Congress alone. If that body will do its duty, relief will come—if not, the Bank feels no vocation to redress the wrongs inflicted by these miserable people. Rely upon that. This worthy President thinks that because he scalped Indians and imprisoned judges, he is to have his way with the Bank. He is mistaken." (Quoted in Catterall, *Second Bank of the United States*: p. 339. Original source not available.) When popular deputations presented themselves to Jackson, he drove them from his presence in rage. As Niles writes, in response to the requests of the Baltimore delegation for relief, he burst out: "Relief, sir! . . . Go to the monster [Second Bank]!—The Government will not bow to the monster." *Niles Weekly Register* (March 1, 1834): p. 9.

9. H. Clay, *Works of Henry Clay* with C. Coltin, ed. (New York: A.S. Barnes, 1855). Clay to Francis Brooke, February 10, 1834.

10. As Biddle expressed it: "What is done at Tammany or at Washington is a matter of little importance to the Bank. The Bank is no longer responsible for the currency, and the people who now have charge of it are welcome to their experiments." *Biddle Papers*, Biddle to Hamilton (February 1, 1834).

11. The only change made by the act of June 24, 1834, respecting the coinage, was to alter the weight of gold coins, giving them 23.2 grains of pure gold and 25.8 standard to the dollar. This changed the fineness to nearly .900 instead of 916–2/3. The resulting ratio was 16.002 to 1. Another act passed the same day provided that foreign gold coins were to be received and pass current at the new ratings which the preceding law established. This act was modified on January 18, 1837, when the prescribed standard of fineness for both gold and silver coins was made .900. The weight of pure silver in the dollar remained the same 371.25 grains; gross weight altered from 416 to 412.5 and fractional pieces changed in proportion. The legal tender power of all silver pieces remained un-

changed. The fineness of gold coins was slightly increased to make it exactly .900. The eagle thus weighed 258 grains of which 232.2 grains were pure gold. This ratio became 15.988 to 1. The difference is so slight that the custom has become universal to characterize the coinage as "16 to 1" thereby ignoring the fractional difference of .012. The coinage of both metals was made free and unlimited.

12. Quoted in *Niles Register*, X, 20. Original source not available.

13. Cf., J. L. Laughlin, *History of Bimetallism in the United States* (Chicago: University of Chicago Press, 1901): pp. 66 ff.

14. *Reports of the Secretary of the Treasury*, III (1837): p. 678.

15. An act of Congress specified that the United States should not pay out bank notes of less than ten dollars after April 14, 1835, and less than twenty dollars after March 3, 1836. Ibid.

16. Ibid.

17. Ibid.

18. Smith, *Economic Aspects of the Second Bank of the United States*, 55 ff.

19. *Reports of the Secretary of the Treasury*, III (1837): p. 764. In certain cases Virginia scrip was acceptable. Moreover, indulgence was granted the small land purchaser (320 acres) until December 15, 1836.

20. How, in fact, this large surplus accumulated in the Treasury may be seen from an examination of government receipts. These receipts show that proceeds from the sale of public lands were the largest item in the government income, after custom receipts. The revenue from customs in 1834 was $16.2 million, $19.4 million in 1835, and $23.4 million in 1836. Annual receipts from government land sales averaged approximately $2.4 million in the ten-year period 1824–33. From 1833 to 1834 land sales amounted to approximately $1 million. By 1835, however, receipts from land sales reached $14.8 million and in 1836 amounted to $24.9 million. In October 1835, total government deposits were approximately $18 million, and by October 1836, $41 million. *Reports of the Secretary of Treasury*, Vol. III (1829–37).

21. *New York Spectator*, December 15, 1836. Open letter from N. Biddle to J. Q. Adams (November 11, 1836).

22. *Hazard's Statistical Register* I: p. 328.

23. *The Secretary of the Treasury*, Vol. III gives the following breakdown: *East*: Maine, New Hampshire, Vermont, Massachusetts, Rhode Island, Connecticut, New York, New Jersey, Delaware, Maryland, District of Columbia, Virginia, North Carolina, South Carolina, Georgia, Pennsylvania, Florida, and the Second Bank of the United States until March, 1836. *Southwest*: Alabama, Louisiana, Mississippi, Arkansas, and Tennessee. *West*: Kentucky, Missouri, Illinois, Indiana, Ohio, Michigan, and Wisconsin.

24. *Reports of the Secretary of the Treasury*, Vol. III, and *Comptroller of the Currency for 1876*.

25. William F. Harding, "State Bank of Indiana," *Journal of Political Economy*, IV (1895): pp. 1–36.

26. Anna J. Schwartz, "Pennsylvania Banking Statistics" (unpublished manuscript, National Bureau of Economic Research).

27. The deposit banks suspended with the rest, and one of the first to yield was the Dry Dock Bank of New York. This was a source of keen chagrin to the administration. The following Treasury Circular is mute testimony to the government-depository relationship: "As the painful information has reached this department through the public press that your bank has suspended specie payments, the object of this letter is to learn, officially, if that fact has happened." *Reports of the Secretary of the Treasury*. Circular letter to depository banks, May 1837. It is interesting that the secretary learned this piece of vital information through the newspapers. The banks were therein notified that no further deposits could be made with them, and what they had would be removed by warrants and transfers, reasonable in amount and time of payment. They were asked further when and how they expected to resume, and what measures they expected to take to secure the government deposits. On May 26, a Treasury order was issued requiring that the public money should be deposited only in banks paying specie: "if there were no such banks, the money should be deposited in those pledging themselves to return the deposit punctually when wanted, in the same kind of money that was placed in them. The deposits not in such banks were to be drawn out and placed in the same."

28. E. G. Bourne, *The History of the Surplus Revenue of 1837* (New York: G.P. Putnam's Sons, 1885): p. 40.

29. Ibid.

30. In the first three months of 1837, exchange rates stood at the specie export point and in April at the time of the second transfer of the surplus to the states, they were above it. The United States lost over $2 million in specie to Britain in the spring of 1837. (*Reports of the Secretary of the Treasury*, Vol. IV [1838]). The loss of specie at this time may be partly attributed to the "adjustment" undertaken by the specie losing country, Britain, in response to the heavy specie outflow which accompanied the capital outflow to the United States in the earlier years. It seems not unreasonable, however, to attribute a part of the specie outflow to a growing distrust on the part of foreign investors in the ability of the United States to maintain the specie standard.

31. Contemporaries denounced the shipment of one million pounds of specie from England to the United States in early 1838 as "mere quackery."

32. *Reports of the Secretary of the Treasury*, Vol. IV (1838).

33. Martin, *Seventy-Three-Year History of the Boston Stock Market*: p. 31.

34. Ibid., p. 31. "These (copper coins) bore all kinds of devices and caricatures, mostly levelled at General Jackson's policy. In the midst of a brisk and lucrative business, orders came from the attorney-general at Washington to prosecute all makers, vendors, and circulators, of spurious coin. . . . Thus ended the fun and profit."

35. *Reports of the Secretary of the Treasury*, Vol. IV (1838), and *Comptroller of the Currency for 1876*.

36. Anna J. Schwartz, "Pennsylvania Banking Statistics" and "New York Banking Statistics" (unpublished manuscripts, National Bureau of Economic Research).

37. R. C. McGrane, *Panic of 1837* (Chicago: University of Chicago Press, 1929): p. 190.

38. Open letter from N. Biddle/J.Q. Adams, *New York Spectator*, April 12, 1838. Quoted in Smith, *op. cit.*: 205. Original source not available.

39. Smith, *Economic Aspects of the Second Bank of the United States*: p. 207.

40. McGrane, *Panic of 1837*: p. 207.

41. S.D. 25th Cong., 3rd Sess., I, pp. 13–14.

42. The Bank, now a Pennsylvania bank, continued to issue notes of the defunct national institution until the government enacted legislation in 1838 making it a misdemeanor for the officers of any institution to issue notes once its charter had expired. Sumner, *Banking in the United States*, vol. I in a *History of Banking in All Nations*: p. 295.

43. Bray Hammond, "The Chestnut Street Raid on Wall Street, 1839," *Quarterly Journal of Economics* (August, 1947): pp. 608–18.

44. J. Cowperthaite to N. Biddle, March 23, 1841. *Hazard's Statistical Register* IV (1841): p. 259.

45. After several attempts at resumption, the Second Bank closed its doors for the last time on February 4, 1841.

46. Hepburn, *A History of Currency in the United States*: p. 164.

Chapter 3

Political and Philosophic Underpinning

A BRIEF SURVEY

A brief examination of American intellectual history provides useful insights into the character and nature of the intellectual apparatus used by Americans to cope and constructively channel bureaucratic and political interaction. The early 19th century struggle for monetary supremacy is but a case in point.

What are the ideas, for instance, that served President Jackson and his followers to undertake what is tantamount to a crusade for monetary reform and against the Second Bank of the United States and its supporters? Recent scholarship suggests that the ideas of classical republicanism strongly influenced the debate. Thus Jackson's war against the Second Bank reflects the classical opposition to "commerce" and that in challenging the "corruptions" of the James Monroe and John Quincy Adams administrations he was attempting to restore "morality" and "virtue" to government.[1]

It is more likely, however, that Jackson and his followers drew on the economic and monetary ideas of John Locke and traditional American ideology than on classical or Scottish philosophy. Consider briefly classical (or better neo-classical) republicanism. It does hold up government as the noblest activity and the concept of a republic based on a balanced constitution and an independent, arms-bearing, property owning citizenry. The idea itself can be traced to the literati of late medieval Italy and their rejection of traditional ideas of scholarly withdrawal and development of a new philosophy urging political engagement and the pursuit of an active life. This philosophy ushered in an attack on imperial rule and a preference for the values of the Roman Republic.

The Florentine literati, in particular, cultivated the ideals of liberty, civic equality and an arms-bearing citizenry. It was Machiavelli, when confronted with what he viewed as a double threat to Florentine liberty in the form of the despotism of the Medici from within and foreign invasion from without, who diagnosed the "corruption" from which the state suffered and prescribed the infusion of "virtue" which was necessary to reinvigorate it.

In his view, "corruption" involved the moral degradation of the individual arising from his pursuit of private interest, his loss of public spirit and his military and political dependence on others. To avoid such a state of affairs, it is necessary to put into place the ideal of a self-sufficient citizen, soldier and patriot. As a property owner the individual would be independent against despotic encroachment while at the same time he would be willing to accept a condition of approximate equality with his compatriots. In sum, the ultimate goal was a well-rounded citizen who would give precedence to the public good, prefer austerity to luxury, and live an unspecialized life, discharging different public functions at different times.

This neoclassical concept of the republic put forth by Machiavelli, according to recent scholarship, can be found in both Whig and Tory thought of the late seventeenth and early eighteenth centuries.[2] And indeed, some scholars argue that this Machiavellian concept is central to the American revolt against the British Parliament and that it served to shape the arguments between the Federalists and Republicans in the 1790s.[3] Moreover, this concept continues to influence contemporary political debate in the view of some scholars.

How did Machiavelli's concept enter into British and American political philosophy? According to Pocock, for instance, Machiavelli's thoughts reached England through James Harrington's *Oceana* (1656).[4] For his part Harrington viewed the end of feudal tenure in England as an emancipation of the free holder. His justification for their military setup in 1649 was that it constituted a classical republic of the armed people, a society of proprietors governing themselves without a class of salaried office holders. Free and frequent parliaments were necessary if so virtuous a regime were to be perpetuated. It was also essential for possession by citizens of the free hold land since commercial or financial forms of property would corrupt their owners by making them dependent on others. One consequence of such a train of thought was to view republican "virtue" and "commerce" as incompatible.

It was not long thereafter (1675) that the Whig opposition "discovered" a republic of land holding warriors in the Gothic past allowing thereby the two myths of classical liberty and the ancient constitution to be brought together into a single synthesis. The synthesis served as a platform from which to oppose eventually the Bank of England and the national debt along with high taxation, ministerial corruption, and a standing army.

Pocock makes the point that establishment of the Bank of England, along with the national debt, provided the turning point of English and Scottish political ideology. The Neo-Harringtonian version of the classical republican myth served those in opposition to the ruling oligarchy. Thus, the creation of public credit came to be viewed as a means for creating dependent relationships which were incompatible with the practice of public virtue. It is this conflict between commerce or "corruption" and virtue that became the primary theme of eighteenth-century social thought and political argument.

Other leading thinkers of the period such as David Hume had little objection to the disappearance of virtuous republics for the simple reason that he considered civilization to be possible without them. He was, however, suspicious of paper credit or paper money as a potentially destructive and unstable force. Josiah Tucker regarded the development of exchange relationships and the division of labor as preconditions of liberty and intellectual progress.

Edmund Burke, however, came into sharp disagreement over the issue made by writers of the Scottish Enlightenment which made commerce the great motor force behind the growth of manners and the progress of society. To Burke, manners and refinement were the creation of the medieval church and chivalry and thus came before commerce and not afterward. With the suggestion, implicit in Burke and explicit in Coleridge that a "clerisy" or educated elite, was necessary to civilize commercial classes, the ideological defense of trade and finance created by the Scottish Enlightenment quietly subsided.

What are we to make of the idea that political thought of the eighteenth century is but a smooth progression from J. Locke to J. Bentham? Not much according to Pocock. He supports the view that Locke's ideas were too radical to be acceptable to the makers of the 1688 Revolution and were largely irrelevant for much of the ensuing century. Bentham simply cannot be put into the virtue/commerce paradigm pushed by Pocock and is simply dismissed by him as an anomaly.

English political thought, in his view, was not dominated by the cold mechanical philosophers of rationalist individualism such as Bacon, Hobbes, Locke and Newton in the eighteenth century. On the contrary, according to Pocock, Whig society was not perceived by its supporters as selfish and materialist. It was philosophically defended on the grounds of its diversity and its capacity to develop the polite together with the mechanical arts.

Eighteenth-century thinkers for Pocock cannot be polarized into aristocratic reactionaries and bourgeois progressives. Indeed there were many points of common interest between Hanoverian lords and the new world of public credit. To defend "commercial" society was to justify the Whig aristocracy. Conversely, the opposition rhetoric of Tory "reactionaries" and radical "progressives" was almost identical.

JACKSONIAN ERA

Certainly classical rhetoric and allusions can be found in the Jacksonian era.[5] Diggins puts it well when he writes, "The image of Jackson as the 'Old Roman,' a man of deep private integrity and personal honor . . . could easily portray Jacksonianism as carrying forth the classical drama of the virtuous many struggling against the corrupt few."[6] In the struggle for monetary supremacy and supremacy over the Second Bank the vocabulary of "virtue" and "commerce" was regularly used.

It is thus not surprising that the use of classical republican vocabulary would prompt scholars to argue that classical republicanism was firmly lodged in America. Howe, for instance, tells us that the continuing use of "virtue, balance, luxury, degeneration, restoration" in the Whig-Democratic debate "reveals the continued influence of long-familiar patterns of classical and Renaissance political thought."[7] A closer examination of the ideological position of Whigs and Democrats during the Jacksonian era, however, suggests that each party had so inverted the charges from the traditional English political position as to make them useless.

As we noted, it was the English landowner who asserted his independence in opposition to the court's influence, which was viewed as corrupting, through positions and pensions, the integrity of Parliament. It was the power of the monarch that was to be resisted because he did not represent the will of the people. In Jacksonian America, however, Diggins tells us that the English Whig tradition of the people against the Crown is no longer relevant because American Whigs were the first to resist the executive branch of government and its powers with the president representing the will of the people. Jacksonian politics met with resistence from the Whigs with its "brokering" among various special interest groups. Jackson made the "spoils system" legitimate through political appointments to ensure that office holders would be dependent upon the executive branch of government "the vice of patronage, the very corruption that English thinkers feared would undermine republics by subverting the moral independence of the citizenry."[8] Moreover, notes Diggins, the Whigs saw themselves as the "heirs of classical politics." For it was Whig ideology that underscored "the need for a mixed government against the threat of executive power . . . the bright idea of progress was always shadowed by the specter of degeneration."[9]

Indeed, the fact is that both sides in the debate used the language of classical politics and they may even have understood each other's accusations and yet it may well be, as Diggins argues, "the language in which the accusations were expressed no longer had any precise or consistent meaning."[10] For using the language of classical politics both Whigs and Democrats would avoid acknowledging what the Federalists candidly admitted: that all parties and factions are "interested" and therefore indifferent to the general good and that no party, faction, class, section, or individual can claim to be acting virtuously. In the Jacksonian era, however, both parties claimed to be acting virtuously, and the idea of "virtue" had no opposite reference to define its meaning, for clearly no party would want to be seen as acting unvirtuously. Thus while the Whigs charged that Jacksonian democracy would issue in a crass plutocracy the

Democrats charged that a coercive plutocracy had already emerged from the "money aristocracy." Similarly, the Whigs attacked Jackson's use of executive power as a form of "tyranny," and Jackson claimed that the Bank of the United States is "itself a government" and that the "distinction between it and the people has become one of power." But to the Whigs the main threat to liberty came not from the power of property but from the power of the presidency; "liberty and the resistance to tyranny had come to mean different things to the Whigs and the Democrats: To the former, liberty meant resisting the tyranny of political power; to the latter, the tyranny of economic power."[11]

In effect no rules of recognition existed that enabled the participants to distinguish who was virtuous and who was not, no understanding and agreement about which participant represented the classical republican principles. Political language was simply at the mercy of its manipulators. Little wonder that "Democrats could justify political patronage and the Whigs private profit—both anathema to classical republicanism."[12]

If language use is inappropriate for judging the course of events during the Jacksonian period for reasons drawn from Diggins, where do we turn for our interpretation? We have discussed in the previous chapter that the struggle for monetary supremacy prompted by political circumstance was an important source of monetary uncertainty. The language and heat of the debate did cast doubt on America's ability to maintain the specie standard. The public sought safety from monetary uncertainty by increasing its holding of specie relative to bank money. This had the effect of producing a smaller increase in the American money stock necessitated by other circumstances (e.g. capital inflow), than would otherwise have occurred. It also produced a smaller rise in the country's general level of prices. The unintended consequence was indeed to promote the government's hard money policy. Though political language may be inadequate in identifying reality, it does nonetheless occasionally produce desired results.

To be sure it may well be, as Diggins argues, that the last thing a political party gives up is its vocabulary. The linguistic lag may well be the result of the tendency on the part of people to shed ideas more quickly than the words used to express their ideas. If not the ideas of classical republicanism as argued by contemporary neoclassical historians, what other ideas are useful for understanding the Jacksonian era? Diggins suggests we turn for useful insights to de Tocqueville who "placed more importance on the structure of class relations than on language systems to explain why (Lockean) liberalism came to pervade American society."[13]

It was Tocqueville who argued that democracies prefer their language obscure. America did not have an aristocracy to pose "virtue" against "commerce." It also lacked a working class to pose the ideals of socialism against individualism "shaped by man's Lockean encounter with nature through hard work in a virgin soil unencumbered by the relics of past regimes of Europe."[14]

And indeed Diggins puts it well when he writes "small wonder that Lockean values would predominate over classical principles and Marxian ideas in an environment that equated property with democracy and promised the individual the natural right to pursue both under conditions of equality . . . if America never had a radical working class capable of making a social revolution, neither did it have a virtuous aristocracy capable of conserving a classical tradition."[15]

The fact of the matter is that the Jacksonian concept of virtue has little to do with classical politics. For Jackson it is the farmers, laborers, mechanics and the like who are basic to the country. He makes a definite distinction between those who "produce goods" and those who "make money." A strong Lockean thread runs through the Jacksonian era as it does throughout American history. A case in point is the Populist movement in the latter 19th century whose members viewed themselves as Jeffersonian yeomen menaced by the international money power.

The traditional republican fears of imperialism, standing armies, and over the corruption of politics by commerce gave way to public concern with the abuses of wealth, capital, property, mortgages, rent, and "unearned income." As Diggins correctly wrote, these concerns are in "the spirit of Lincoln and Paine and the labor theory of value central to Lockean liberalism."[16]

Diggins writes that American populism emerged as a struggle between the "the people" and "the interests" or the honest worker versus the rich and aristocratic. Like Jacksonianism, late nineteenth century populism, with its roots in a Lockean-mounted attack, was against all of the economic forces that could possibly deprive citizens of their right to ownership and opportunity "a new form of 'tyranny' represented in the rationalizing principle of industrial capitalism—'the trust.' "[17]

And, indeed, it was John Adams and Mark Twain, for instance, who asked us to look behind the language of politics for real motives and interests. No particular group or individual had a monopoly on virtue and honesty. For the historian Vernon Parrington, the corruption of American politics came through business and commerce. He hailed the writings and efforts of Dewey, Veblen, Beard, Theodore Roosevelt, and Wilson for their "dramatic discovery" of the source of corruption.

Why then did not the Progressives push forth with the classical republican tradition and return the American republic to its "first principles"? Diggins argues that the Progressives thought there were two traditions in American political thought that caused the problem. According to Beard, liberalism did not survive the Constitution because Madison's controls not only frustrated popular will but allowed corporate power to prevail in a political culture already dominated by interest politics. Calvinism, Parrington believed, provided a "native" theology justifying wealth and making capitalism legitimate—the result: Material success became a sign of moral virtue to distort the meaning of Calvinism and Liberalism. Classical political ideas could have been a hope for the future, but scholars didn't give much meaning to "political virtue."[18]

One can argue that the nature of the American character is such that it will neither consent to the commands of the state nor to the convictions of the past. Thanks to its Lockean tradition America was beyond the reach of classical political thought. The pursuit of self-interest is as natural to Americans as nature itself.

It is this characteristic, in particular, that made Americans unique in the eyes of many foreign observers. Unlike Europeans, for instance, Americans looked neither to the political state nor to the system of class relations to provide a sense of identity, to an organic hierarchy that promised social harmony or to a class movement that promised social justice. Americans had neither the experience of a subordinate position to the state nor a class structure through which the individual may achieve a sense of self.

It may well be that the solutions to America's political and social problems are frustrated by what Diggins calls the "beginning of liberal individualism and liberal pluralism." Indeed, if liberalism can be defined as the overthrow of authority and the search for its substitute, as Walter Lippman puts it, then the search can be endless.

The fact is that Lockean and Calvinist sentiments, as Diggins argues, can be found to be compatible in the minds of leading American thinkers and leaders and are useful in gaining insights into American issues including monetary issues. To the extent that Locke had believed, for instance, that the fruits of one's labor could only be preserved by "money," the one "lasting thing" that could prevent the spoilage of value in goods, suggests from whence Jacksonians drew inspiration for their drive for "hard money" and against paper bank money which could be easily manipulated. And certainly the Lockean ethos nurtured the belief that protection of private property is the basis of all American rights.

In the view of leading Jacksonian thinkers such as William M. Gouge, influential writer on monetary and banking affairs, a man has as strong a natural right to the profits which are yielded by capital which was formed by his labor as he had to the immediate product of his labor. He believed that wealth should be a reward for industry and thus advocated monetary and banking reform that would minimize the role of private banks to assure equity and justice for all who honestly earned their wealth. In his view bank credit and paper money reduced Americans into overextending their investing and consumption so that they became dependent on banks which themselves were subject to economic cycles that required that loans be periodically recalled. Moreover, the existing American banking system, in his view, led easily to political corruption by means of bribes to gain and retain permissive state bank charters.

And the Lockean labor theory of value that pervaded Jacksonian culture also had roots in the seventeenth century Puritanism, eighteenth century liberalism and early nineteenth century utopian and Christian Socialism. The Calvinist doctrine of New England Puritanism not only stressed the doctrine of the calling through which man serves God by honest labor of all forms but also justified property with basis of work and made waste as sinful as idleness. Lockean philosophy would easily build on Puritan theology. It is natural that the doctrine of work as it developed in American history became closely related to the concepts of virtue, liberty and progress. The decline of classical values in America can be in good measure attributed to its ascendancy.

Classical political thought did little to promote the value of labor. In fact, in Greek and Roman thought, labor was scorned and consigned to slaves and the majority of men and women whose thoughts and actions could never arise from the private realm to join with minority—the elite—to engage in the pure, contemplative exercise of mind, art, philosophy and politics. This is very unlike the philosophies of such diverse thinkers as Locke, Karl Marx and Adam Smith.

Indeed Adam Smith argued that a commercial society was fairer than that of the ancient republics because it was more productive. The division of labor enabled modern economies to break out of the inexorable cycle of luxury, corruption and decline; they could achieve self-sustaining growth, under which even the wage laborer would enjoy a better living than that of the property-owning citizen of the classical republic.

To be sure the true nature of early American republican thought remains an open question. It appears more than that the Federalist polemic of Thomas Jefferson and James Madison of the 1790s was simply a replay of political arguments in England. American political thought does appear to be much more than simply another version of classical republicanism. The Americans of the Jefferson-Jackson vintage did in fact reject the elitist implications of civic humanism and asserted an economically progressive definition of freedom as the right of all men to the enjoyment of property and participation in an expanding commercial system. And for his part Madison strongly upheld the view that a stable monetary system not easily manipulated brings about increases in the country's real wealth.[19]

Indeed, the Founding Fathers like Adam Smith saw man as a creature of "self-love" and thus incapable of behaving in a disinterested manner. They distrusted the pretension to altruism and benevolence of all classes, and thus Adams and Madison placed checks on Hamilton's "rich, well born, and able." Even Jefferson who equated the "pursuit of happiness" with economic independence saw clearly the heart of the matter: "Take from man the selfish propensities and he can have nothing to seduce him from the practice of virtue."[20]

The *Federalist* authors saw social behavior as even more troublesome than individual behavior which could at least be subject to individual conscience and public response. We should not expect from various groups or "factions" that pride or shame will serve as constraints because people acting collectively do not reflect critically upon their actions. In group behavior egoistic impulses are magnified particularly when individuals composing the group see themselves acting virtuously.[21]

NOTES

1. See J. G. A. Pocock, *The Machiavellian Moment: Florentine Political Thought and the Atlantic Republican Tradition* (Princeton: Princeton University Press, 1975); Robert Remini, *Andrew Jackson and the Course of American Freedom*; Daniel W. Howe, *The Political Culture of American Whigs* (Chicago: University of Chicago Press, 1979); J. G. A. Pocock, *Virtue, Commerce and History, Chiefly in the Eighteenth Century* (Cambridge: Cambridge University Press, 1985).
2. See especially the work of J. G. A. Pocock.
3. See references cited in note 1.
4. J. G. A. Pocock, *The Ancient Constitution and the Feudal Law: A Study of English Historical Thought in the Seventeenth Century* (Cambridge: Cambridge University Press, 1957).
5. See John Patrick Diggins, *The Lost Soul of American Politics: Virtue, Self-Interest, and the Foundations of Liberalism* (New York: Basic Books, 1984), Chapter 4.
6. Ibid.: 106–107. See also Arthur Schlesinger, Jr., *The Age of Jackson* (New York: Little, Brown, 1945) for earlier documentation on the use of classical language during the Jacksonian period.
7. Daniel W. Howe, *The Political Culture of American Whigs* (Chicago: University of Chicago Press, 1979): p. 78.
8. Diggins, *The Lost Soul of American Politics*: p. 11.
9. Ibid.
10. Ibid.
11. Ibid., pp. 111–12.
12. Ibid., p. 113.
13. Ibid., p. 114.
14. Ibid., p. 115.
15. Ibid., p. 116.
16. Ibid., p. 123.
17. Ibid., p. 124.

18. Ibid., p. 130.

19. See Ralph Ketcham, *James Madison: A Biography* (New York: Macmillan, 1971): p. 175.

20. Quoted in Diggins, *The Lost Soul of American Politics*: p. 339.

21. Thus, Diggins writes that "the framers of the Constitution" began with the assumption that man's desire to tyrannize others was so ingrained that he must be restrained. The classical idea being that virtue "implied the strength to resist temptation," with man knowing right from wrong, which gives him the moral freedom to make his choices.

Chapter 4

Traditional American Ideology and Money

LOCKEAN LIBERALISM

Classical and Scottish political philosophy has been drawn upon not only to offer an alternative to Lockean liberalism but also to explain the American Revolution and much else, as this study underscores. To be sure the extent to which John Locke influenced the Founding Fathers is an on-going debate among historians. Lockean liberalism is underscored by some scholars as the very foundation of America: such Lockean tenets as man's natural right to economic as well as political liberty, the government's obligation to protect property, the people's opportunity to pursue material happiness. Other scholars who deny the liberal tradition also tend to deny as invalid or irrelevant Locke's philosophy of individualism.[1]

Nevertheless, it was Lockean liberalism that served and indeed still serves as an important plank in America's philosophical platform. Indeed where else could Americans turn for language to declare their independence but to John Locke, that "all Men are born free and independent." The American Declaration of Independence hailed man's freedom and autonomy. Thomas Jefferson certainly did not conceive of man as a communal creature whose mind depended upon the bonding presence of others. In his view the same spirit of autonomy applied to political units as well as to discrete individuals. To Jefferson the individual and his rights must be sacrosanct. All this is in marked contrast to Scottish thought which emphasized man's sociability and dependency and belief that moral consensus of society took precedence over private interests and conscience. So too is Locke's view—and shared by

Jefferson—at odds with classical politics which emphasized the overriding importance of the public good.

American fear that they would be turned from respectable independent citizens into abject dependent slaves has remained a predictable constant in the country's political affairs. Such emotions have worked against a communal political culture, having been derived from servitude, not being born free, according to de Tocqueville, who claimed that Americans have to work their way up from "involuntary" labor.[2]

It is little wonder that Locke has such a profound impact on American affairs. When his works are taken as a whole, he clearly articulated what has become traditional American ideology. Indeed, George C. Lodge argues that such American political figures as President Ronald Reagan, Senator Barry Goldwater and President Gerald Ford, among others, are the more recent representatives of this traditional ideology and which breaks down into five great ideas articulated by Locke in the seventeenth century:

1. *Individualism*—the atavistic notion that the community is no more than the sum of its parts;
2. *Property rights*—the guarantee that the individual will be free from the predatory powers of the sovereign;
3. *Competition*—the means of controlling the uses of property to serve individual consumer wants;
4. *The limited state*—a government lacking authority to plan or interfere significantly in economic life but capable of responding to crises or interest group pressures;
5. *Scientific specialization and fragmentation*—the theory that if we attend to the parts, as experts and specialists, the whole will take care of itself.

LOCKE ON MONEY

Consider briefly Locke's views on money. As we know, his purpose in economics was to clear up what he considered confusion about the interest rate and the price level.[3] To this end he found it useful to present a general theory of value which provided a basis for a theory not only of money as a medium of exchange but also of interest, rents, and capital values.[4] Accordingly, his discussion of money can be considered in three parts: origins of money; the requirements and functions of a money commodity; the determinants of the value of money. The first two are important in setting out his philosophy and attitude toward money while the third is his quantity theory of money.

Money has its origin, in Locke's view, in man's desire to exchange his surplus of perishable commodities for more durable commodities which would be preserved for long periods of time without deterioration. Although any durable commodity would suffice, gold and silver are particularly suitable because of their indestructibility, durability, and ability to maintain their value. Over time these metals acquired a store of value and people began accepting them in exchange for other commodities thereby establishing them as an exchange medium. The net effect has been for the two functions to reinforce each other thanks to the suitability of the two metals as a store of value which made them acceptable to people in exchange, and their ready acceptance in exchange for commodities which made them more reliable as stores of value. Thus by placing an imaginary value on otherwise worthless commodities man, according to Locke, acquired a very useful instrument for bridging the past, present, and future. In effect, money came about through an implicit contract which enabled people to overcome the difficulties inherent in the state of nature. Such an origin of money well serves Locke's contract theory of the origins of society.

According to Locke and to many other people before him the money commodity must be durable, divisible, universally acceptable and scarce in order for it to function properly as money. On this score gold and silver are the most suitable money commodities as a ready comparison will illustrate. Lead, for instance, is too abundant and too prone to rapid changes in price to be a money commodity. For political reasons Locke excludes paper money, which is readily manipulated, and he views token money as little better than fraud. Although no ordinary metallist, Locke is certainly a "hard currency" proponent to whom President Andrew Jackson and his followers could turn for inspiration and theoretical guidance.

It is in Locke's determinants of the value of money that a version of the quantity theory of money is to be found. Accordingly, the demand for money as a medium of exchange will be stable, not be subject to the same forces as other commodities. In effect, the velocity of money is stable so that the value of money is determined by the quantity available. Since the value of money is the inverse of the general level of prices for goods and services, an increase in the quantity of money increases the price level and vice versa. Unlike earlier "quantity theorists," Locke's theory focused on the function of money as a medium of exchange and not simply as an empirical explanation of an existing inflation or deflation based on supply and demand analysis.

All that is necessary to make Locke's "quantity theory" recognizable today is simply to interpret the money side of the equation as a flow rather than a stock. There is a rate of turnover or velocity of circulation of money that also plays a part in determining the value of money. There is much to suggest that Locke did indeed recognize this aspect of his theory.

THE QUANTITY THEORY OF MONEY: VELOCITY AND CASH BALANCES APPROACHES TO MONEY

The quantity theory of money set forth by John Locke is now a shared monetary heritage for which philosophers as distant as Law, Hume, and Aristotle are called in evidence. Its more recent advocates include Irving Fisher and Milton Friedman. Its basic proposition is that inflation results from too much money chasing too few goods.

For instance, Professor Irving Fisher's (1867–1947) perhaps best known contribution to the field of money is the equation of exchange which is usually expressed as MV = PT.[5] The equation is a simple statement of identity, although it is often confused with the quantity theory of money. It states that the quantity of money (M), multiplied by the average number of times each unit of money is used during a given period (V), is equal to the sum total of goods and claims traded (T) during the period, multiplied by the average price (P). Since the equation is not a theory but an identity, it provides no basis for prediction. As a consequence, it is not open to disputes as to its "truth" or "falsity". The only problem, if any, presented by the equation of exchange is its usefulness as an analytic framework.

On the criterion of usefulness, a modification of the equation of exchange restricts transactions to those involving real income (y) and a price level (P_y) corresponding to this income. Thus $P_y y_y$ represents total money income or receipts. By dividing total money income by M, income velocity (V_y), or the average number of times each unit of money enters into income in a given period of time, is obtained. The corresponding identity becomes:

$$(1)\ MV_y = P_y y$$

This modification of the equation of exchange or, as it is usually called, the "Income-Velocity" approach has the advantage of ready availability of statistical data on income and prices.

These identities are converted into theory and are capable of providing a basis for prediction by making various assertions about the terms in either the equation of exchange or income velocity approaches. Assertions about the various terms, however, also result in more than one version of the quantity theory of money. Thus, it is that in answer to the question of what determines price level changes, the "rigid" version of the quantity theory is simply changes in the stock of money. A looser version of the theory asserts that price levels are the consequence of a combination of three factors: the quantity of money, its rate of turnover, and the balance of transactions or income. Both versions of the theory, however, accept the assertion that the price level is passive. Consider the quantity theory view of money's effect on output and interest rates.[6]

Money's Effect on Output

Nominal money refers to the money stock or the actual dollar (dinar, pound, franc, etc.) amount of money (currency and deposits) in the economy. Real cash balances, on the other hand, can be thought of as the total dollar amount of money adjusted for changes in the price levels. If, for example, the nominal money stock stays constant but prices double, the amount of real cash balances in the system can be thought of as declining by 50 percent. The quantity theorist assumes that the nominal quantity of money can be controlled by the monetary authorities, but that the amount of real cash balances is determined by activities within the economic system.

The relationship between changes in nominal money and changes in real cash balances lies at the heart of the quantity theory. Increasing (decreasing) the rate of growth of the money supply is hypothesized to leave households and businesses with excess (deficient) cash balances. People have three options in disposing of these excess funds: (1) they can use a portion of them to purchase credit instruments; (2) they can use them to purchase goods and services; and (3) they can do both. Increasing the demand for goods and services will affect prices; however, this will affect the level of real cash balances.

The extent to which an increase in nominal money leads to an increase in real cash balances depends on the extent to which prices change. Generally speaking, in periods of high unemployment, such as during a recession, increasing the amount of nominal money would be expected to increase aggregate demand and output of goods and services relatively more than prices. On the other hand, when the economy is fully employed in, for example, a "boom" period, increases in the amount of nominal money would be expected to lead to an increase in prices.

Money's Effect on Interest Rates

The second major aspect of the quantity theory is the relationship between changes in the nominal quantity of money, prices, and interest rates. To explain this relationship, quantity theorists like to talk about three effects of changes in the rate of growth in the money supply on interest rates: (1) the liquidity effect, (2) the income effect, and (3) the price anticipation effect. The magnitude of each of these effects and the time lag before they are felt, depends, in part, on how fully employed the economy's resources are.

The first effect to be felt is the liquidity effect. This results from increasing (decreasing) the rate of growth of the money supply leaving households and businesses with more (less) money than they wish to hold. Increases cause them to shift some portion of these excess balances into credit instruments, increasing the price of these instruments, therefore, decreasing interest rates. According to the quantity theorists, increasing the stock of money will also lead to an increase in the demand for goods and services. This, in turn, will tend to stimulate, after a three- to six-month lag, the demand for credit by businesses and households. This increased demand for credit, which is called the income effect, leads to a decline in the prices of credit instruments and an increase in market interest rates.

In addition, the quantity theorists say, the increased aggregate demand for goods and services will tend to increase prices. The amount of inflation, however, depends upon the extent to which resources are employed. More importantly, as households and businesses begin to feel the effect of inflation, they may tend to expect more of it. This, in turn, will add to the credit demand. If people expect prices to increase and if interest rates are low, it is logical that they will want to go into debt.

The increase in the demand for credit caused by inflationary price expectations leads to the price anticipation effect on interest rates. Lenders also come to expect inflation and, therefore, require a higher return to compensate for the expected loss in purchasing power.

As a result of this price anticipation effect, quantity theorists like to speak of interest rates as being made up of two parts: One portion of the interest rate relates to the "real" return on capital assets (assuming no expected inflation), while the second portion relates to changes in expected prices.

Let us assume that an individual anticipates no inflation and receives a 4 percent return on his investments. Now let events change and assume he anticipates 3 percent inflation to continue indefinitely. It is hard to expect this individual to be content with his 4 percent return. Instead, he will want the 4 percent he was receiving, plus 3 percent additional to compensate for the expected inflation. Market interest rates reflect these price expectations.

This theory explains the often-heard contention by quantity theorists that increasing the money supply, while admittedly decreasing interest rates in the short run (the liquidity effect), will eventually lead to higher interest rates (the income and price effects). Because quantity theorists believe that the economy is inherently stable, they contend that the real rate of interest, as opposed to the market price of interest, does not change very much. Most of the changes therefore, that are observed in the market rate of interest result from erratic historical changes in the money supply.

Much of the criticism of the quantity-velocity formulation of the quantity theory rests on challenging the basic assumptions underlying the theory, especially in its more rigid form. Neither velocity nor income nor transactions, it is argued, are stable. All are subject to rapid change even in very short periods of time. Velocity changes at times may be an even more important factor than the quantity of money in accounting for short-run changes in the level of prices.

Another criticism deals with the passive nature of the level of prices. It is asserted that P, far from being passive, may in fact contribute to changes in the other factors. For example, a rise in the level of prices may encourage people to dispose of their money for fear that its purchasing power will decline even further. Such disposals are registered in an increase in velocity.

Moreover, under a specie-standard, a change in prices may affect the production of the monetary metal and so the stock of money (M). A rising level of prices may increase the costs of producing specie and conversely for a falling level of prices. The net effect is that P is not necessarily passive and may even influence M—albeit after a considerable period of time.

Milton Friedman's reformulation of the quantity theory of money freed it from dependence on the assumption of automatic full employment. The emphasis is on the role of money as an asset. He treats the demand for money as part of capital or wealth theory concerned with the composition of assets. On Friedman's reformulation, it is important to distinguish between ultimate wealth-holders to whom money is one form in which they choose to hold their wealth, and enterprises to whom money is a producer's goods, like machinery or inventories.

MONETARISTS, AUSTRIANS, AND KEYNESIANS

Milton Friedman identifies "monetarism" with the quantity theory of money, suggesting thereby that monetarism is not a new development.[7] The principal tenet of "monetarism," as in the quantity theory of money, is that inflation is at all times and everywhere a monetary phenomenon. Its principal policy corollary is that only a slow and steady rate of increase in the money supply— one in line with the real growth of the economy—can ensure price stability.

Milton Friedman [*The Counter-Revolution in Monetary Theory*, First Wincott, Memorial Lecture (London: Institute of Economic Affairs, 1970)] summarizes the monetarist view on the relationship between the money supply and the price level in the following:

1. There is a consistent, though not precise, relation between the rate of growth of the quantity of money and the rate of growth of nominal income;
2. This relationship is not obvious to the naked eye—largely because it takes time for changes in monetary growth to affect income. How long this process will take is within itself a variable;
3. On the average, a change in the rate of monetary growth produces a change in the rate of growth of nominal income about six to nine months later. This is an average which does not hold in every individual case;
4. The changed rate of growth in nominal income typically shows up first in output and hardly at all in prices;
5. On the average, the effect on prices comes about six to nine months after the effect on income and output, so the total delay between a change in monetary growth and a change in the rate of inflation averages around 12 to 18 months;
6. Even after allowances for delays in the effect of monetary growth, the relation is far from perfect, for there's many a slip "twixt the monetary change and the income change";
7. In the short-run, which may be as much as five or ten years, monetary changes affect primarily output over decades, although the rate of monetary growth affects prices primarily.

The "monetarist" view, as summarized in Friedman's *Counter-Revolution*, in effect questions the doctrine advanced by Keynes that variations in government spending, taxes and the national debt could stabilize both the price level and the real economy. This doctrine has come to be called "The Keynesian Revolution."

It is to the "Austrian School" and through such members as Carl Menger, Georg Simmel, (actually a sociologist), Ludwig von Mises, and Friedrich von Hayek, that useful insights are had into the monetary system as an integral part of the social structure. Their views differ significantly from both Keynesian and monetarist views, though Milton Friedman and some monetarists come closer to the Austrians in their emphasis on "monetary rules" and a stable monetary order.

According to the Austrian view, money and the monetary system is the unintended product of social evolution in much the same fashion as the legal system.[8] Money is a social institution—a public good. It is not simply another durable good held in the form of "real balances" by utility maximizing individuals or profit maximizing firms as Keynesian and monetarist views hold. However useful the tools of demand and supply analysis applied to money as a private durable good, Keynesians and monetarists miss the full consequences of monetary instability.

In essence, the monetary system is an integral part of the social fabric whose threads include faith and trust which makes possible the exercise of rational choice and the development of human freedom. This is misunderstood by the very people who benefit from it. It is this misunderstanding of the social role of money as a critical element in the market mechanism and the need for confidence in the stability of its purchasing power that came to dominate much of Keynesian and monetarist monetary thought in the postwar period. This misunderstanding is the ideological key to the use of discretionary monetary policies for monetary expansion as an unfailing means of increasing output and employment and reducing interest rates.

Herbert Frankel writes that Keynes, following Georg Friedrich Knapp, presents the monetary system as a creation of the state and as such available for manipulation by government consisting mostly of wise and well-educated people disinterestedly promoting the best interests of society. The fact that such an arrangement curtails individual choice and decision did not disturb Keynes who saw little reason to believe that those choices and decisions benefit society. In essence, it is at best an elitist view of government so familiar to Great Britain at the turn of the century or at worst a totalitarian government on the model of the Soviet Union.[9]

David Laidler takes exception to Frankel's argument that Keynes is the architect of a short-run monetary policy that seeks to exploit monetary illusion in order to trick people into taking actions which, if they could correctly foresee their consequences, they would not take. Such "trickery" is not the policy product of the 1930s when Keynes believed that undertaking an activist monetary policy to deal with unemployment would be what individual agents desired but were prevented from accomplishing on their own because of price and market mechanism failures. Keynes, in effect, thought he was dealing with the issue of involuntary unemployment. It was in the 1950s and 1960s that the idea of a stable inflation-unemployment trade-off generated a "money illusion" available for exploitation by policy makers. I have argued elsewhere that such policy availability also assisted in the pursuit of the cold war as well as the Vietnam War with indifferent results to produce much of the recent world-wide inflation and sped the entrance of the "Third-World" as an outstanding world problem.[10]

In my view, Laidler is correct that policies derived from Keynesian philosophy of money may not be the fundamental reason that faith in the institutions of a free society is threatened. Though, again, the policies of the 1950s, 1960s, and 1970s do owe much to Keynes' followers, if not to Keynes himself. These policies did indeed fool the population into providing more labor services and resources which did permit the Western world to compete with the Soviet Union and its friends while presenting an aura of prosperity at home. Keynes did provide the theoretical apparatus to make possible the articulation of his post-World War I vision. It was in the late 1970s and 1980s that the "chickens came home to roost," so to speak, with the era of rational expectations and growing distrust of government.

The inter-war collapse of the international economy can be attributed more to unforeseen political factors than to often-cited economic factors.[11] In essence, the British Empire collapsed taking with it its role as a world stabilizer. The United States, the only other world power of sufficient strength to act as a stabilizer, refused to do so with predictable consequences.

The rise of socialism in the 1930s promoted central economic planning and redistribution of income policies. The Keynesian Revolution stressed the failure of the economic system which was avoidable by the application of scientific knowledge. Harry Johnson is surely correct when he writes that these two movements reinforced one another.[12] In turn, this led to the view that economic backwardness can be traced to defects in the private enterprise system, not to the backwardness of people and their cultures in relation to the requirements of modern industrial society. The "Third World" promoted this view to the top of world's development agenda since the 1960s in the form of demands for a "New International Economic Order" (N.I.E.O.).

In drawing on Georg Simmel's view for a free and stable monetary order, Frankel does not take into sufficient account the above largely political factors. As a result, he attributes too much responsibility to Keynes and his followers for the lack of faith and trust in the "old order." The free monetary order that underpinned Simmel's turn-of-the-century society can be defended on moral grounds as "an ideal—the pursuit of trust." The durability of the old order was questioned by Simmel, as Frankel points out, long before Keynes and his followers appeared.

Its durability is questioned by Simmel throughout his *Philosophy of Money*. This study is concerned not simply with money as a unit of account, a store of value and medium of exchange, but with the free market economy in which the monetary system is an integral part, and the relationship between the institutions of such an economy and the matters of justice, liberty and the nature of man as a social being. The focus is on exchange as one of the most fundamental functions which serves to tie individuals into a cohesive social group. Since barter exchange is inconvenient, there naturally developed a group of individuals who are specialists in exchange and the institution of money which serves to solve the problem of the dual coincidence of barter. As soon as money enters the picture and the dual coincidence of barter is resolved, exchange ceases to be a simple relationship between two individuals. Simmel notes that the ensuing generalization of claims made possible by money-transfers places these claims for realization upon the general economic community and government as its representatives.

Unlike other things that have a specific content from which they derive their value, money derives its content, according to Simmel, from its value. Its value in turn owes much to the implicit guarantee given by society and the community and little to the physical properties of money. It is, in effect, based on the confidence in the sociopolitical organization and order. In this view, the British pound sterling, formerly, and the American dollar, currently, owe their value more to the political and economic power and prestige of their institutions than to the physical properties of the pound and dollar. This confidence in the political and economic institutions of a country that Laidler, Rowe, and Frankel attribute to Simmel (in translation) is "trust."

"Trust" then is the cement of society and the more of it individuals have in a society's institutions in general and in its money in particular the more extension and deepening in the use of money will occur in an economy. By and large the consequences of such developments are beneficial to society in that man's achievements are enhanced not only in the economy but in all other endeavors. Indeed, freedom and justice are promoted by the development and growth of exchange and the monetary economy.

As a consequence, the individual is enabled to act independently of other individuals while at the same time becoming more dependent on society as a whole. That is, an individual becomes more dependent on the achievements of individuals and less so on the peculiarities of personalities. The loosening of bonds serves to promote economic freedom. It may or may not promote political freedom at the same time.

Simmel underscores two likely sources of trouble for a free monetary order, which are serious enough to threaten the survival of the order. First, the receipt of money wages instead of payment in kind while promoting individual freedom exposes the recipient to the uncertainties and fluctuations of the market originating in turn in fluctuations in the purchasing power of money. Secondly, the very success of the free monetary order also encourages the development of socialist ideas which serve to undermine the individualistic order based on free markets and money. Laidler, Rowe, and Frankel underscore Simmel's concern about fluctuations in general and inflation in particular since the uncertainty so generated undermines trust in the monetary order.

In fact, Laidler's evaluation of the significance of the "Austrian" view of money is basically correct. If money is taken to be one among a complex of social institutions, one consequence of inflation is to move the social order away from the use of money and towards a greater reliance on greater government control in various forms or command organization. Such a development, Laidler notes, increases the dependence of individuals on other "specific personalities" and less on freedom—so much for anticipated inflation.

In unanticipated inflation, the "Austrian" view foresees an increase in uncertainty inherent in a money economy that could undermine mutual trust which is essential for monetary exchange. The net effect would be a decline in the number of mutually beneficial exchanges taking place. Since monetary instability and market failure are closely linked in the "Austrian" view, both anticipated and unanticipated inflations serve to weaken the social fabric.

Laidler and Rowe write that "if monetary theory is best approached along Austrian lines, then we must conclude that mainstream monetary theory, for all its considerable accomplishments, not only trivializes the social consequences of inflation in particular . . . but that it grossly underestimates the destructiveness of monetary instability in general. . . . Note that we here refer to modern monetary theory and not to its proponents. The principal authors of 'shoe leather' approach to analyzing the cost of inflation, such as Friedman, have expressed far more concern about the importance of controlling or avoiding inflation than their theories could possibly justify, as their opponents (e.g., James Tobin, "Inflation Control as a Social Priority" 1977 cited by Laidler and Rowe) have been quick to point out. In this their instincts have, in our view, run far ahead of their analysis" [Laidler and Rowe, "Georg Simmel's Philosophy of Money: A Review for Economists." *Journal of Economic Literature* (March 1980): 102].

According to Laidler and Rowe, Keynes, too, was concerned with monetary stability and the fragile nature of a money-using market economy and the social order that went with it. He was also well aware of the need for "trust" in the stability of purchasing power if the market mechanism was to function properly. Indeed, to Keynes money is not just another commodity. A money economy is very different from a barter economy. This idea was lost, write Laidler and Rowe, "as the Hicksian IS-LM (Investments/Savings-Liquidity Money) interpretation of the *General Theory* came to dominate monetary economics—'monetarist' as well as so-called 'Keynesian'. The dominance of this incomplete version of Keynes in subsequent debates has surely been the main reason for participants in them having neglected 'Austrian' ideas on these matters" (Laidler and Rowe: 103).

The story, however, is very different on the conduct of monetary policy where Keynes and his followers depart significantly from the Austrian and monetarist paths. These differences are so profound as to overwhelm areas of agreement. As we discuss in this study, Keynes believed firmly in discretionary monetary policy and viewed the gold standard as a relic. Modern Austrians hold to the gold standard. The monetarists argue for a given growth rate in the stock of money. The difference between the Austrians and the monetarists is essentially about means to achieve agreed upon ends, though the latter do not stress the role of stability in promoting "trust" and so facilitating the functioning of markets. The Austrians, while distrusting the bureaucrats, are more skeptical than monetarists about the stability of the demand for money function and so argue for pegging the price of money in terms of gold relying on the stability of the relative price of gold in terms of goods in general.

Frankel, in his study *Two Philosophies of Money*, directs attention to the erroneous "nominalist" theories of money which imply that money is something external to the fabric of society, a thing or commodity in its own right, which governments are entitled to manipulate in pursuit of their own limited economic or social ends. He draws and compares the views of Simmel and Keynes arguing that both understood the economic uses and psychological power of money. Simmel and Keynes were also sensitive to its resultant influence on human character and behavior. More important perhaps Frankel demonstrates how the views of Simmel and Keynes summarize the conflicting ideologies of the nineteenth and twentieth centuries and serve to place in perspective contemporary monetary problems. According to Frankel, "It arises out of the conflict between money as a *tool* of state action and money as a *symbol* of social trust. The two concepts are incompatible. I go so far as to contend that for several decades we have been witnessing an intense reaction against traditional concepts of monetary order: it is not far removed from a revolt against it."[13]

The traditional view of money focused on a free monetary order which "implies the possibility for individuals of choosing between a multiplicity of conflicting goals or ends. It postulates the existence of principles, enforced by customs, convention and law, which ensure that its operation will not be arbitrarily, capriciously, or lightly altered in favor of particular groups, individuals, or interests."[14] The real nature of the monetary debate argues Frankel "is basically not about inflation or deflation, fixed or flexible exchange rates, gold or paper standards and so forth, it is about the kind of society in which money is to operate."[15]

The survival of the free monetary order is questioned because it might not prove possible to make it work in terms of specific goals which society should, in their opinion, pursue. This view, shared by Keynes, leads to utopian attempts to make the uncertain certain by control of society according to plan as well as by transformation of man.[16] This is reflected, writes Frankel, "in the ongoing highly sophisticated debate about the scope, legitimacy and effectiveness of monetary policy. On the one hand, there are the optimists who believe that we now possess the technical tools and scientific knowledge to enable us to control monetary behavior, not only within a nation, but even internationally, and thereby not only the rate of economic change, but progress also. On the other hand, their opponents would support Friedman's view that "We are in danger of asking it to accomplish tasks that it cannot achieve and, as a result, in danger of preventing it from making the contribution that it is capable of making."[17]

To use the monetary system to pursue changing goals and objectives is incompatible with monetary order, argues Frankel. It will make it "capricious and uncertain and prey to conflicting and varying political objectives."[18] Intended to reduce uncertainty, monetary manipulation actually increases it by casting in doubt the monetary system itself. A monetary policy, writes Frankel, "which is directed to shifting goals . . . as for example, full employment, economic growth, economic equality or the attempt to satisfy conflicting demands of capital and labour . . . cannot but vary with the goals adopted."[19]

According to Frankel, it is, Keynes who made the revolt against the predominant nineteenth-century view of money respectable. It was George Simmel—especially in *The Philosophy of Money* (*Philosophiedes Geldes*) first published in 1907 in Berlin—who first suggested the sources of the revolt and foresaw its likely consequences. In essence, Simmel does not see the institution of money in mechanical terms but, as Frankel writes, "a conflict between our abstract conception of money and the social trust on which it rests. He was concerned to elucidate the moral basis of monetary order in contrast to the subversion of morals through money, in the abstract, which he feared" (p. 5). And Simmel is pessimistic that the free monetary order will survive the revolt against it.

The nineteenth-century view of society's responsibility to maintain trust and faith in money was supported by the bitter eighteenth-century experiences with currency excess. Most classical economists and certainly the "Austrians" underscored society's monetary responsibilities for preserving trust and faith in money. Simmel's contributions to monetary thought are in keeping with the spirit of the tradition. It is against the use of discretionary monetary policy for the purpose of exploiting the presumed short-run non-neutrality of money in order to increase permanent employment and output by increasing the stock of money. Though an arbitrary increase in money, according to Simmel, will not necessarily disrupt relative prices permanently, such manipulation sets into motion forces whose consequences for social stability are very serious indeed. Since no human power can guarantee against possible misuse of the money issuing authority, to give such authority to government is to invite destruction of the social order. To avoid such temptation, it is best to tie paper money to a metal value established by law or the economy.[20]

Of course, Keynes, too, was essentially a monetary economist. His writings are an integral part of our received monetary heritage. Certainly his work, *Monetary Reforms*, draws on this heritage while at the same time adding to it.[21] It was also Keynes who told us in 1919 in his *Economic Consequence of the Peace* that there is no better means to overturn an existing social structure than to debauch the currency.[22] He also alleged that Lenin indeed espoused that the best way to overthrow the capitalist system was to debauch the currency. And, ironically, some can argue that it was also Keynes' subsequent teaching which opened the flood gates of inflation in the post-World War II period even though he personally attempted to close these gates shortly before his death in 1946.[23]

Keynes clearly shared a monetary heritage common to Simmel, the Austrians, and the monetarists. What sets him apart, of course, is his views on the conduct of monetary policy. Friedman, for instance, writes that where he disagreed with the views Keynes expressed in *Monetary Reform* is with the appropriate method for achieving a stable price level. Keynes favored managed money and managed exchange rates—that is, discretionary control by monetary authorities.[24]

It appears that it is the exercise of discretionary policy by monetary authorities advocated by Keynes that underscores his differences with the monetarists and Austrians. Setting aside the monetary role of gold as a barbarous relic casts him in disagreement with the Austrians. His desire to place the execution of monetary policy at the discretion of public spirited and competent civil servants sets him in disagreement with monetarists who argue for growth rate rule for some definition of the money supply. But some of these differences cast Keynes out of our received monetary heritage.[25]

NOTES

1. John Patrick Diggins, *The Lost Soul of American Politics: Virtue, Self-Interest and the Foundations of Liberalism* (New York: Basic Books, 1984): pp. 32ff.

2. Ibid., p. 35.

3. Karen Iversen Vaughn, *John Locke: Economist and Social Scientist* (Chicago: University of Chicago Press, 1980).

4. Ibid., p. 31.

5. Irving Fisher, *Purchasing Power of Money* (New York: Macmillan, 1911); Don Patinkin, *Money, Interest and Prices* (Evanston: Row Peterson, 1965); Robert L. Hetzel, "The Quantity Theory Tradition and the Role of Monetary Policy" *Economic Review*, Federal Reserve Bank of Richmond (May/June 1981): pp. 19–26; Milton Friedman, ed. "The Quantity Theory of Money—A Restatement," *Studies in the Quantity Theory of Money* (Chicago: University of Chicago Press, 1956): pp. 3–21; David Meiselman, ed. *Varieties of Monetary Experience* (Chicago: University of Chicago Press, 1970); Milton Friedman and Anna J. Schwartz, *A Monetary History of the United States 1867–1960* (Princeton: Princeton University Press, 1967).

6. Milton Friedman, "Money: Quantity Theory, II," *International Encyclopedia of the Social Sciences*, Vol. 10 (1968); A. G. Hart, "Money: General, I," ibid.; R. T. Selden, "Velocity of Circulation, III," ibid.; Milton Friedman, "The Optimum Quantity of Money" in *The Optimum Quantity of Money and Other Essays* (Chicago: Aldine Publishing Co., 1969): pp. 1–50; D. H. Robertson, *Money* (London: Nisbet, 1948); George Macesich and H. Tsai, *Money in Economic Systems* (New York: Praeger Publishers, 1982).

7. "I would say that personally I do not like the term 'Monetarism,' " writes Friedman, "I would prefer to talk simply about the Quantity Theory of money, but we can't avoid the usages that custom imposes on us." Milton Friedman, "Monetary Policy: Theory and Practice," *Journal of Money, Credit and Banking* (February 1982): p. 101.

8. R. T. Selden, "Monetarism" with Sidney Weintraub, ed. *Modern Economic Thought* (Philadelphia: University of Pennsylvania Press, 1976): pp. 253–274; T. Mayer "The Structure of Monetarism," *Kredit und Kapital*, VIII, Nos. 2 and 3 (1975): pp. 190–218, 293–316; Thomas Mayer, *The Structure of Monetarism* (New York: W. W. Norton and Company, 1978); George Macesich and H. Tsai, *Money in Economic Systems* (New York: Praeger Publishers, 1982): Chapter 12; L. Anderson, "The State of the Monetarist Debate," *Federal Reserve Bank of St. Louis Review* (December 1978); A. J. Schwartz, "Why Money Matters," *Lloyds Bank Review* (October 1969); George Macesich, *The Politics of Monetarism: Its Historical and Institutional Development* (Totowa, NJ: Littlefield and Adams, 1984); George Macesich, *Monetarism: Theory and Policy* (New York: Praeger Publishers, 1983). See also G. P. Dwyer, Jr., and R. W. Hafer, "Is Money Irrelevant?", *Federal Reserve Bank of St. Louis Review* (May–June 1988) (St. Louis: Federal Reserve Bank of St. Louis, 1988): pp. 3–17. The authors conclude that the evidence for the period 1979–84 is consistent with the monetarist view.

9. David Laidler and Nicholas Rowe, "Georg Simmel's Philosophy of Money: A Review Article for Economists," *Journal of Economic Literature* (March 1980): pp. 97–105; S. Herbert Frankel, *Two Philosophies of Money: The Conflict of Trust and Authority* (New York: St. Martin's Press, 1977) and review of Frankel's study by David Laidler in *Journal of Economic Literature* (June 1979): pp. 570–572; S. Herbert Frankel, *Money and Liberty* (Washington, D.C.: American Enterprise Institute for Public Policy Research, 1980).

10. George Macesich, *The International Monetary Economy and the Third World* (New York: Praeger Publishers, 1981): Chapters 1–2.

11. Ibid.

12. Ibid., Chapters 2–3.

13. Harry Johnson, "The Ideology of Economic Policy in the New States," D. Wall, ed. *Chicago Essays on Economic Development* (Chicago: University of Chicago Press, 1972): pp. 23–40.

14. S. Herbert Frankel, *Two Philosophies of Money: The Conflict of Trust and Authority* (New York: St. Martin's Press, 1977): p. 86.

15. Ibid., p. 4.

16. Ibid., p. 95.

17. Ibid., p. 6.

18. Ibid. and Milton Friedman "The Role of Monetary Policy" in *The Optimum Quantity of Money and Other Essays* (Chicago: Aldine Publishing, 1969): p. 99.

19. Frankel, *Two Philosophies of Money: The Conflict of Trust and Authority*: p. 89.

20. Ibid., p. 92.

21. Georg Simmel, *The Philosophy of Money* (Translation by T. Bottomore and D. Frisby, with Introduction by D. Frisby) (London and Boston: Rutledge and Kegan Paul (1977, 1978): p. 160. He writes, "The most serious repercussions upon exchange transactions will follow from this situation, particularly at the moment when the government's own resources are paid in devalued money. The numerator of the money fraction—the price of commodities—rises proportionately to the increased supply of money only after the large quantities of new money have already been spent by the government, which then finds itself confronted again with a redeemed supply of money. The temptation then to make a new issue of money is generally irresistible, and the process begins all over again . . . temptation whenever money is not closely linked with a substance of limited supply. . . . Today we know that only precious metals, and indeed only gold, guarantee the requisite qualities, and in particular the limitation of quantity; and that paper money can escape the dangers of misuse by arbitrary inflation only if it is tied to metal value established by law or by the economy."

22. John Maynard Keynes, *Monetary Reform* (London: Harcourt Brace and Co., 1924).

23. John Maynard Keynes, *Economic Consequences of the Peace* (London: Macmillan, 1920).

24. F. A. Hayek, "The Keynes Centenary: The Austrian Critique," *The Economist* (June 11, 1983): p. 39.

25. Milton Friedman, "A Monetarist Reflects: The Keynes Centenary," *The Economist* (June 4, 1983): p. 19.

Chapter 5

Renovating American Ideology and the Monetary Organization

PERCEIVED SHORTCOMINGS OF LOCKEAN LIBERALISM

Georg Simmel identifies two likely sources of trouble for the human institution of money. One source is that since individuals do not receive income in kind but rather in money, they are exposed to the uncertainties originating in fluctuations in the purchasing power of money. The other is that the very success of a free monetary order encourages the development of socialist or collectivist ideas which serve to undermine the individualistic order based on free markets and money.

Monetary uncertainty will tend to move the social order away from the use of money and markets towards a greater reliance on one form or another of greater government control or command organization thereby strengthening bureaucracy and its political influence. Furthermore, monetary instability and market failure are closely linked and both serve to weaken the social fabric.

In our discussion of the Jacksonian era and the monetary uncertainty which characterized that turbulent period in American history, individuals attempted to protect themselves by converting paper money into gold and silver. They were encouraged to do so as a matter of federal government policy. In the process, however, the country was also deprived of the benefits of a uniform paper currency in the form of the bank notes of the Second Bank of the United States and that of other viable and sound banks. It is not altogether certain that Simmel would have approved of such a "hard money" policy. In his view the best course is to tie paper money very firmly to gold if we are to avoid the failures of arbitrary issues of paper money. On the other hand, with the aversion to paper money in mind, Locke would have found it easy to support the "hard money" policies of Jackson and his followers.

The very success that the American economy enjoyed by the mid-nineteenth century brought into question the free monetary order upon which that success was based. While economists and others were stressing the important role played by money as a medium of exchange, a standard of value, or a store of wealth, other thinkers and writers regarded money as alienating and wealth a corrupting force in political life. New England Transcendentalists are but a case in point in depicting the shortcomings of Lockean liberalism.

In fact, many an American thinker in the years before and after the Civil War began to view the political philosophy of John Locke as defective because it made property the very expression of man's being. For some American thinkers the highest expression of man lies not in acquisitive activity but in nature itself. To really understand nature, Americans, in their view, should turn to Greek and German idealism or indeed to Eastern mysticism.

Ralph Waldo Emerson writes that history is but the work of ideas, and Locke's definition of man is transformed in not what he produces but what he perceives. History, argues Emerson, is simply the work of ideas. Emerson is praised by many people as a man of ideas who deals with causes rather than effects. Ideas were viewed by him as means whereby inspired feelings could produce thoughts to liberate America from the bonds of Lockean materialism and the chains of Calvinism.[1]

The alienation of American intellectuals from political institutions can best be understood as a reflection of history and philosophy. It is a result, argues Diggins, of "American writers repudiating the past to liberate the mind. . . . New England Transcendentalism and Western liberalism . . . offered antithetical modes of perceiving reality . . . thus the Federalists settled for moderation, tolerance, compromise and pluralism. The Transcendentalists . . . identified the essence of man with his mind, intellect, and 'Oversoul' . . . liberation of the citizen from all constraint . . . independent of all others and dependent only upon the spontaneous promptings of one's own mind . . . only one sin, the curse of both Calvinism and liberalism—prudence."[2]

Though sensitive to effects of economics on morality and the idea that prosperity would always undermine republics, Emerson nonetheless did not subscribe to the solution of contemporary socialists nor to the exponents of classical thought. His basic aim was to show Americans how they could pursue profits without losing their souls. To Emerson America was the exception and could avoid the fate of the Old World by thinking correctly about the meaning of work and the ends of life.

His economic philosophy differs from Locke who valued property as the fruit of man's mixing his labor with the materials of earth, from the socialists who saw man as producing the conditions of material life because of economic necessity and from classical theorists who believed governmental institutions and civic consciousness could subdue the forces of corruption that emerge in an economy of trade, credit and commerce. For Emerson conscious thought is the source of all productive activity. Indeed, money cannot be an alienating medium since it, too, is a production of the human spirit. Man cannot be alienated from what he produces and creates. For Emerson the basis for political economy is noninterference by the state. The safest rule is to allow supply and demand to adjust without state legislation and/or intervention. Social unity can evolve from economic competition if man transcends his narrow self-interest and renounces all that is low and vulgar. For Emerson, in effect, money, trade and commerce were liberating not threatening. No government intervention is necessary. In his view, the capitalist is seen as a moralist working upon matter. Politics and government should be so reduced so that each man can become a state unto himself.

For Henry Thoreau, on the other hand, wealth was neither a symbol of aesthetic activity as Emerson argues, nor the fruit of energy and enterprise as Alexander Hamilton believed, nor the means whereby virtue is undermined as classicists would argue. It signified, in his view, an illusion of happiness in the pursuit of a phantom in the fashion of Jefferson's Lockean idea of happiness. Economic activity as such is for Thoreau little more than gambling where the risk taker bets the present against the future.

His departure from Emerson is straightforward. He condemned

all human desires for wealth and power. For Thoreau the pursuit of wealth stunted man morally and led to the exploitation of life by making economic activity the very definition of life. It is also a singular departure from the Lockean philosophy with its emphasis on money, property and labor. At the same time, Thoreau's views have little in common with the Marxist critique of alienated man and bourgeois society or for that matter with Adam Smith's philosophy of laissez-faire. In his view it was man himself who was strangled by society's conventions. Alienation and corruption for Thoreau was simply human "meanness," man's refusal to transcend his own egoism.[3]

Thoreau considered the fundamental American problem to be "the illusion of political freedom and the reality of economic passion and interests."[4] The drive and energy which Emerson believed would lead to "genius" and "power," Thoreau considered as undisciplined impulses that never result in the cessation of desire. Both grasped that politics and ethics may be inherently incompatible and power and virtue inherently contradictory. As Transcendentalists they asked little of government and much of man. Men made their own institutions rather than institutions making men. All this is in marked contrast to classical thinkers who believed that although human nature may not change, human conduct can be constrained and uplifted through the design and construction of proper political institutions. It also contrasts with the view of Locke and Jefferson that man's passions should be directed at nature while political institutions should protect men from each other.

Money, in Thoreau's view, was a source of trouble since it comes between man and his objectives. It was, in effect, alienating as Simmel and other writers argue later including nineteenth century Marxists who saw the idolatry of money as a species of "reification," an "illusion that led man to believe that he could possess through wealth what he had lost through work—his essence and being."[5]

As America developed during the course of the nineteenth century, such writers as Henry Adams and Frederick Jackson Turner raised concern over the future of the American Republic. Unlike de Tocqueville, Henry Adams seems to have uncovered corruption everywhere in the America of his day. Money not only corrupted politics but the state itself. Abraham Lincoln called upon Americans to embrace the ideals of the Declaration of Independence and Christian mores.

Henry Adams, the great-grandson of John Adams, one of the *Federalist* authors, considered the American theory of government a "failure" and the Constitution itself as "expired," for it was not able to control economic power by establishing political authority. The development of new forms of corporate power simply could not be controlled along the lines and with the mechanisms emphasized by the *Federalist* authors. If the central government is to provide effective control over these new forms of corporate power, it needed more power which was expressly denied it by the country's basic laws, and if granted such power, the central government would sooner or later fall into the hands of those it was attempting to control. Adams observed that the United States would either move into the future with an expanded central government in order to better cope with the growth of corporate power, or if it remained true to the basic principles of its Constitution, Americans would find themselves unable to cope with the new reality of corporate power.

THE MONETARY ORGANIZATION: NATIONAL BANK ACT OF 1863–65

The American monetary scene in the period beginning with the Civil War, including the National Bank Act and the eventual establishment of the Federal Reserve System in 1913, is but the monetary manifestation of the beginning of centralization and communitarianism with its idea that if the community is well-designed, its members will have a sense of identity with it. This is a period which shaped the country decisively and laid the groundwork for a strong central government. Critics of Lockean liberalism served to inspire these changes.

The character of post-Civil War reconstruction was basically political and economic in which the country's monetary and financial organization served as a principal instrument of policy for the push toward centralization. Not everyone, of course, supported these developments. Again, as in the Jacksonian period, strictly domestic events were played out on a broader international scene.

In the process, Lockean liberalism tended to be moderated if not replaced by the idea of community.

Three principal objectives were to be served by the passage of the National Bank Act. First, the United States was to be provided with a uniform and par value currency. Bank note detectors and state bank notes would henceforth find places in museums and histories of quaint Americana. Second, the market for government bonds would be enhanced thereby providing means to finance the war and sustain the government's credit after the war. Third, the Act would effect an improvement in general banking operations. The more flagrant abuses in commercial banking would at least be arrested by depriving banking institutions of a number of adventurous outlets. The mercantile tradition of banking—the "banking principle"—was to be the dominant philosophy under which banks operated.

Drawing freely from previous banking experience, especially that of New York State, the Act provided that any five people who could raise the necessary capital might start a bank. These banks were authorized to have their own notes printed by the Comptroller of Currency who issued them to the national banks in return for a deposit of government bond with the Secretary of the Treasury. Banks also were required to deposit with the Secretary an amount of government bonds equal to one-third of their capital stocks. If more notes were desired for circulation, they could be issued provided the bank deposited an additional amount of government bonds, and that such an issue did not increase the bank's note circulation beyond its paid-in capital stock. Total notes authorized were $300 million. These were apportioned regionally and were expected to fill the vacuum left by the anticipated retirement of state bank notes, and (possibly) United States notes.

Banks chartered under the 1863 Act were known as "national banks" because of their national charters. Other features distinguished them from most banks chartered by the various states. National banks in seventeen key ("reserve") cities were required to maintain cash reserves amounting to 25 percent of note and deposit liabilities; 15 percent was required for all other banks. Although these national banks were permitted to conduct regular commercial lending, they were prohibited from lending on real estate or on their own stock. Furthermore, when a national bank failed, government bonds on deposit with the Secretary of Treasury were used to pay off the bank's note circulation in full. In order to reinforce this provision the government had first claim on all remaining assets thereby insuring full reimbursement by the Treasury of the failed bank's notes. No longer would the American people, and foreigners as well, suffer from banking "adventurers."

However, any cheering at this state was premature, for victory was not yet complete. Although the National Bank Act provided for conversion of state banks into national institutions, many of these state institutions were understandably "backward" in serving the interests of the public when they felt that their own interests were jeopardized. A more positive measure was required to speed their entrance into the national banking fraternity. Such a measure was passed in 1865 when Congress levied an annual tax of 10 percent on the outstanding note circulation of state banks. So effective was this measure in taking the profit and adventure out of state banking that by 1866, the number of national banks had increased rapidly; state bank notes soon went out of existence. While many state banks became national banks due to the goad of the tax, many more simply avoided the tax by substituting deposit liabilities for the note liabilities they had lately issued. Demand and time deposits from this time on (1867) were a predominant fraction of the total money stock. Deposits were about equal to bank notes in 1860.

At the time of their secession in 1861, the Confederate states had 189 of the country's 1,862 banks, and their banking system was about on par with the rest of the country. For various reasons southern bankers showed remarkable restraint in creating bank notes and deposits during the war.[6] Undoubtedly a sizeable portion of the $825 million increase in outstanding Confederate government notes occurring between 1860 and 1864 entered the banking system where these notes added to the South's banking reserve. Yet bank notes and deposits in the same period expanded only by three times.

Eugene Lerner correctly argues that one of the principal reasons for the southern bankers' restraint is that they had no central bank to turn to during a crisis.[7] They expected mass withdrawals whenever federal troops approached. In order to protect themselves, southern bankers resorted to credit restraint and a build-up in their reserves. Some indication of the size of these reserves is provided by Lerner in support of his argument. Georgia banks held 47 percent reserves in June 1862, and 69 percent in June 1863; the Bank of Fayetteville, North Carolina, held 21 percent in May 1861 and 46 percent in November 1863; the Bank of South Carolina held 5 percent in January 1861 and 30 percent in October 1863; the Bank of the Valley in Virginia held an average of 41.2 percent in 1861, 56.5 percent in 1862, 57.2 percent in 1863, and 66.4 percent in 1864.

In fact, Lerner estimates that as of January 1864 only $1.20 of bank money was created per dollar printed by the government. Northern banks, on the other hand, created $1.49 for every dollar printed during the war by the government—almost 25 percent more than the southern states.[8]

Though restraint is indicated on the part of southern bankers, the same cannot be said for their government. The Confederate government returned readily to the monetary tradition and practices of the American Revolutionary War and taxed via the printing press by issuing Confederate notes. Indeed, from July 1, 1861, to October 1, 1863, 68.6 percent of all the revenue entering the Confederate treasury came from the printing press.[9] "No one," writes Lerner, "planned to finance this way. Because it was so financed, inflation became inevitable."[10] The method of financing the war, however, is consistent with earlier American traditions.

This does not mean that attempts were not made to hold inflation in check. When the Confederacy's currency reform took hold in May 1864, and the stock of money declined, the general level of prices also declined. And, significantly, the decline in prices occurred in the face of military, political and economic disaster. Unable to collect taxes and sell bonds, the Confederate government turned once again to the printing press, with the result that prices once again began to increase and continued until the end of the war.

The large drain of manpower into the army during the first two years of the war caused a "once and for all" drop in the South's real output.[11] Blockade and Union armies further reduced the region's output. By the end of the war, the South, for all practical purposes, emerged as an economic wreck.

If the Confederate government voluntarily turned to monetary radicalism and methods of government finance popular during the Revolutionary War, the Union victory went even further and forced the South into "colonial" monetary status from which it did not recover until the twentieth century. The National Bank Act of 1863 passed during southern absence, and the annual 10 percent tax on issues of state bank notes are in no small measure responsible for subsequent southern difficulties. Needless to say, the federal government did not provide for the establishment of a development fund nor a bank through which resources could be channeled for economic development of the South and which would compensate it for the losses arising out of economic integration.

POST–CIVIL WAR PROBLEMS IN THE MONETARY ORGANIZATION

The National Bank Act solved two technical problems in the currency. It made bank notes uniform in design and gave them parity of value. One major fault that remained was the so-called seasonal "inelasticity" of the currency, a trouble spot that plagued the economy throughout the nineteenth century. Neither the reformers nor their opponents were clear on the meaning they attached to the word "elastic." If by "elastic" they meant a ready conversion from one form of money to another, their solution was relevant. If on the other hand they interpreted "elastic" to mean responsiveness of the total means of payment to the "needs of trade," they were not addressing the problem of the total money supply.

The national banks could issue currency and hold government deposits if they put up government securities as collateral. Since the fiscal policies of the government generally called for reduction of the national debt and a falling price level in order to further the resumption of specie payments, the government bonds available as collateral for national bank note issues were gradually withdrawn. The remainder appreciated in value. To a large extent national bank notes were held as reserves by non-national banks, so their issue or retirement had the multiple effects that resulted from any change in bank reserves. In essence, the banking system had several "layers": the national banks in reserve cities, other national banks, and non-national banks. The larger banks were generally national and they not only issued bank notes that the country banks used for reserve, they also accepted deposit accounts of the country banks during the seasons in which the demand for bank credit was generally dull. Thus, some of the national banks had certain central banking overtones: they issued notes and held reserves of their correspondents. They primarily differed from a central banking system in that they failed to hold liquid reserves of sufficient volume to provide emergency reserves for the layer of national and non-national country banks. Instead of holding some "excess" reserves for use in strategically critical periods, they extended their credit "on call," anticipating a twenty-four hour return in liquid form when their country correspondents in turn "called" them. Frequently loans on call could not be liquidated, the interior banks could not then get their necessary reserves, and bank panics and depressions were triggered. These actions and reactions provoked suggestions for centralization of the reserves of the banking system and for creation of a liquidity source that would provide bank reserves and currency in accordance with the seasonal demands for credit.

Even though the permissible volume of national bank notes had been increased to $354 million in 1870, and "reapportioned" so the South and West could have more, the currency and bank reserves to many banks remained secularly and cyclically inelastic. Agitation for relief came from two principal sources: the Greenbackers and the Free Silverites. Both of these groups favored "cheap" money; that is, they opposed the resumption of specie payments at the pre-Civil War content of the gold dollar. Both groups were part and parcel of the same movement, a movement against the necessary decline in the price level required for a return to the gold standard. Before silver was discovered in large enough quantities to provide generous increases in the money stock, greenbacks were their lever for amelioration of the price level. Greenbacks, however, were obviously fiat, were obviously not "sound," and were not dignified with monetary value. Monetized silver could meet all these objections and therefore became the vehicle for monetary expansion after 1875.

Clearly fiat money could be made as elastic as popular opinion wished. Advocates of "sound" money therefore had to find some antithesis to the strong (if not inflationary) medicine of the cheaper money advocates. Their actions were rear guard during the 1870s and 1880s. First, greenbacks were not retired as originally intended but statutorily fixed at $356 million (1878). Second, the law prescribing resumption of specie payments was passed in 1875, but in order to obtain it "free" banking also had to be permitted. For every restrictive monetary measure, some compensating, "easy money" relief had to be granted. Under "free" banking and specie standards, currency and deposit issues could be as elastic as the metallic supply and the needs of business would dictate.

Sound money men had also to give in on the monetization of silver. Limited monetization made prices relatively buoyant in the 1880s. When the gold standard was threatened in the middle 1890s, either silver monetization had to stop or the silver standard had to be adopted exclusively. Mankind in the words of gold standard opponents was "crucified on a cross of gold." Fortunately, fresh gold discoveries in the Klondike and South Africa turned the cross into a magic carpet. Indeed the period from 1898 to 1914 is referred to as the "Golden Era."

The "sound" money group were thus forced to retreat on secular issues. Their philosophy for seasonal elasticity, however, was a reaffirmation of the real-bills, commercial paper-only doctrine. Government, they argued, was in no position to impute any elasticity to the currency it might issue because it was out of "touch with business." Only banks that had such a "touch" by way of business loans could assure an elastic currency. Competition among banks and prompt specie payments would make such a currency automatic or self-regulating.

Other sources of irritation in the operation of the National Bank Act of 1863 also caused agitation. Collection of out-of-town checks was a particularly trying task. No centralized or clearing system for checks was available. In order to avoid exchange charges banks relied on their correspondents for check clearance. Such a practice saw checks drawn on nearby banks traveling hundreds of miles from correspondent to correspondent before finally reaching their destination.

Some provisions of the National Bank Act had the result of excluding New York City as an international financial center even though it was. The Act prohibited national banks from accepting drafts drawn on them either by foreign or domestic merchants.

London banks continued to finance the bulk of American foreign trade, and London maintained its position as the world's leading financial center.

Even more serious were the monetary problems inflicted upon the South in the post-Civil War period. The South was not included in the initial apportionment of $300 million in national bank notes. A substitute of a sort for these notes was effectively destroyed in 1865 when Congress levied an annual tax of 10 percent on the outstanding note circulation of state banks. This was a singular disaster for a people that attached such importance to having a currency, even a depreciating one like the Confederate dollar, that they were willing to pay a great amount of resources for it. So great was the price in fact that it enabled the Confederate government to finance almost 70 percent of the war effort by currency issues. The resulting monetary squeeze facilitated the economic stagnation that characterized much of the South in the post-Civil War period. Thomas C. Cochran reports that in every southern state, the 1880 level of per capita income originating in commodity production and distribution is below, or at best slightly above, that of 1840.[12]

Some idea of the monetary squeeze in the South may be obtained from scattered evidence readily at hand in *Historical Statistics* and in the *Comptroller of Currency Report for 1876*. In 1861 in the six principal southern states (Virginia, North Carolina, South Carolina, Georgia, Florida, and Alabama), total bank loans and discounts amounted to $85.4 million, state bank note circulation $42.2 million, and deposits $18.8 million. For the same six states in 1876, loans and discounts for all national banks amounted to $19.2, national bank note circulation $9 million, deposits $10.9 million, and holdings of U.S. government securities as security for notes and deposits amounting to about $11 million. If state banks in the South maintained the same relationship to national banks as in the rest of the country in the same period, the estimates for loans and discounts would be increased by a third. It is not likely that the gap was completely filled by U.S. notes (greenbacks), although the total amount outstanding was $378 million in 1865 which rose to $441 million in 1876.

Unfortunately, we lack a definitive study of how the circulating media of the United States actually flowed into the South following the war. Theoretically we should expect to observe that the South generated a favorable balance of trade with the remainder of the country or received an inflow of such currency from capital imports into the region. In any event a principal generating industry for a favorable balance of trade was undoubtedly that for which the region had a comparative advantage, namely, agriculture. And it is also the industry least likely, in terms of its credit needs, to receive a favorable hearing before the adherents of the "real-bills" doctrine. Various discriminatory devices, such as unfavorable railroad rates and basing point systems erected largely by northern economic interests probably worked against the development of a broader industrial base in the South. The net effect was that the South entered the twentieth century in possession largely of a declining industry which further intensified and complicated the region's economic, political and social problems. It is little wonder that the South, like the early American colonies, became fertile ground for all sorts of "cheap money" ideas and separatist schemes. For all practical purposes the South once again assumed a "colonial" monetary status.

It is difficult to quantify the South's losses from subsequent integration with the rest of the country. Undoubtedly the operation of the National Bank Act and its feature of making U.S. bonds security for note issues intensified the South's problems. In the first place, requiring national banks in the South to hold U.S. bonds as collateral for note issues had the effect of transferring capital desperately needed for reconstruction out of the region. In the second place, actions of the U.S. government after 1880 had the effect of curtailing national bank notes by drastically reducing the profitability of their issue. This profitability depended on the price of the U.S. bonds eligible to serve as collateral. After 1880 the Treasury began to purchase bonds in the open market thereby raising their prices and thus reducing the profitability of issuing notes. The surplus which made such purchases possible came from increases in customs revenues and at the expense of the South's free trade sentiments.[13] Phillip Cagan estimates that when from 1864 to 1880 these bonds sold at or just above par the issuance of notes returned an excellent profit. According to his calculations a rate of return of 31 percent was realized in 1879 in capital tied up in issuing notes. By 1882 this return dropped to 9 percent and in subsequent years fell even below the average rate of return on other assets. As a consequence, the total quantity of outstanding notes was sharply curtailed. Thus, at the beginning of the decade of the 1880s the amount outstanding was about $300 million and at the end of the decade it dropped to about $126 million expanding again in the 1890s when premiums on U.S. bonds fell sharply.

Although these purely domestic monetary events had important effects on the South's prostrated and underdeveloped economy as well as on the general economy of the country, they are but a part of a larger picture framed within the confines of the international specie standard. Even though the United States was *de facto* off the specie standard and on flexible exchange rates during the Greenback period and its return to the specie standard in 1879, no benefits could be expected from such an arrangement because the country was politically and psychologically attached to the specie standard and fixed exchange rates. In the period 1873–1896 all countries on the specie standard experienced a deflation which reflected inadequate growth in the world gold stock. The discovery of gold and its increased production after 1896 was reflected in a general world-wide price rise. If the United States was to adhere to the specie standard and fixed exchange rates, little freedom for independent monetary action existed. No course was open but for the country to participate in the world-wide deflation and subsequent inflation. Internal monetary affairs once again became largely a manifestation of external events that only served to intensify the devastated South's already serious problems. It is but one manifestation of integration by currency convertibility on the specie standard.

Flows of gold gave the whole world years of prosperity after 1898. In the United States gold was made the only legal tender in 1900. The share of new gold this country was getting solved the secular inelasticity in the supply of money for the time being, but seasonal variation became even more of a problem. When Secretary of the Treasury L. M. Shaw used the powers of the Treasury to meet this problem his advice was much criticized as governmental meddling in business. The panic of 1907 seemed to verify the allegations that Treasury influence in the money market was aggravating rather than relieving monetary problems. What was wanted was a stand-by agency: one that would mobilize and centralize bank reserves and do so automatically with some easily understood sound business rules.

The institution later developed to satisfy these demands was the Federal Reserve System. The only constraints the member banks faced in obtaining an "unlimited" volume of Reserve bank credit were: (1) the quality and type of commercial paper they presented, (2) the rate of discount they had to pay, and (3) the gold reserve restriction the Federal Reserve Banks themselves faced in supplying such credit.

In sum, the Jacksonian vision of government in dealing with monetary affairs was confirmed and extended into the American banking and financial community. To be sure, doubts about an activist state grew during the latter part of the nineteenth century as the Republican Party was transformed from an ideological movement pushing for a powerful and beneficent national state into an organizational party more worried about patronage and power than lofty principles.

This transformation began with President U. S. Grant who had his own problems with the American economy and colorful but politically debilitating scandals. It accelerated with the election of President R. B. Hayes. More than a generation would pass before the federal government again would seek an activist role in monetary affairs.

NOTES

1. Diggins, *The Lost Soul of American Politics*: p. 195.
2. Ibid., pp. 196–7.
3. Ibid., p. 216.
4. Ibid., p. 217.
5. Ibid., p. 210.
6. Ibid., p. 170.
7. Milton Friedman, "Prices, Income and Monetary Changes in Three Wartime Periods," *American Economic Review* (May 1952): p. 635.
8. Eugene M. Lerner, "Inflation in the Confederacy," *Studies in the Quantity Theory of Money*, Milton Friedman, ed. (Chicago: The University of Chicago Press, 1956): p. 169.
9. Ibid.
10. Ibid., p. 175.
11. Thomas C. Cochran, "Did the Civil War Retard Industrialization?"

Gerald C. Nash, ed. *Issues in American Economic History* (Boston: D.C. Heath and Company, 1964): p. 293.

12. It also made possible the payment to Union veterans of a very handsome sum of over $2 billion in pensions before 1880–1900. The Arrears Act of 1879, moreover, meant that every Union veteran who was disabled in 1880 was typically assumed and easily proved to have been disabled in the War and thus received a lump sum payment for the fifteen years between 1865–1880. Such veterans' payments in the 1880s amounted to over $650 million. Needless to say, in all of these considerations, the southern veterans were left out. I am indebted to my former colleague, Professor W. P. Dillingham, for these observations.

13. See also the discussion of this period in Milton Friedman and Anna Jacobson Schwartz, *A Monetary History of the United States, 1867–1960* (Princeton: Princeton University Press, 1963) especially chapters 2 and 3; James K. Kindahl, "Economic Factors in Specie Resumption: The United States 1865–79," *Journal of Political Economy* (February 1961): pp. 34–35; and Rendigs Fels, *American Business Cycles 1865–1897* (Chapel Hill: University of North Carolina Press, 1959); Lawrence H. Officer, "The Floating Dollar in the Greenback Period: A Test of Theories of Exchange Rate Determination," *The Journal of Economic History* (September 1981): pp. 629–50.

Chapter 6

Ongoing Debate: Managed Capitalism

THE DEBATE AND ISSUES RAISED

In a letter to William Allen White in 1937, Walter Lippman, considered by many people to have been America's political conscience for better than fifty years of the twentieth century, writes that

> The idea which I had in my mind in writing the book [*Good Society*] was that our present troubles originated in a wrong turn taken by human thought about the middle of the last century. . . . We might hope, perhaps, to change the direction of the current a little in our [time] but no one can hope to see the results in his day, for according to my calculations it takes about sixty or seventy years for a change in fundamental ideas to express itself in public life. Our generation is hopelessly entangled in the errors of the late Victorians.[1]

The good turn taken in the seventeenth and eighteenth centuries in his view is in the principle that the politics, law and morality of the Western world are an evolution from religious conviction that all men are persons and that the human person is inviolable. That this is in fact a good turn most people will agree. Most people will also agree with Lippman's other observation that the continuing industrial revolution posed all the great issues of the epoch that arise primarily from the increasing division of labor in ever widening markets. Over a lifetime Lippman attempted to resolve these vexing issues.

The wrong turn which he rejected is the "gigantic heresy of an apostate generation," and its mistaken belief in authoritarian principle and collectivist state as the key to resolving problems arising out of harnessing modern technology. This mistaken belief grew out of the confusion about the development of "concentrated corporate capitalism" which he considered a transitory and correctable distortion of the free market. Indeed it was the functioning of the free market which brought about the improvement in man's condition.

In his view the movement toward collectivism was fed on the nonsense issued forth by people who erroneously equated the free market with *laissez-faire* government. This self-serving view represented freedom for monopolies but really corrupted the free market. Control for themselves over monopolies was sought by the reformers and labor leaders because they firmly believed in (1) no restraint for popular majorities in their continuing demands for an increased government role; (2) drive to dominate in the private system of corporate collectivism; and (3) no desire to disband monopolies and privilege. "They became the adversaries of freedom and the founders of the new authoritarian society."[2]

For supporting evidence Lippman drew on the experience in the Soviet Union, Nazi Germany and Fascist Italy wherein absolutism was the outgrowth of the essential principle of a full-blown collectivist society. "All collectivism . . . whether . . . communist or fascist, is military in method, in purpose, in spirit. . . . The tragic irony of the time: The search for security . . . if it seeks salvation through political authority, ends in the most irrational form of government . . . in the dictatorship of casual oligarchy."[3]

Collectivism, he argued, also perverted nationalism which at first served to overcome the particularism of petty states. Nationalism later became a reaction against the free market and in favor of protective tariffs to provide special protection to favored groups and government interests. These favored interests and groups promoted and pushed forth collectivism which favored insulation of the state from its neighbors. Indeed, he went on, "collectivism moves toward anarchy, the totalitarian state toward isolation."[4]

In the collectivist state, Lippman contended that the rulers used terror tactics to control the masses through indoctrination that the real enemy was the privileged nations, not the privileged people at home; "the proletarian became imperialist. Thus arose the dreadful prospect of total war . . . fought not for specific objects but for supremacy."[5] Here, he observed, he had succeeded in relating domestic and foreign policy organically one to another.

Lippman promoted not the liberalism of laissez-faire but the liberalism of a compensatory state. It is the first principle of liberalism, in his view, that the market must be preserved and protected. To this end he advocated outlawing monopoly; provision of equal bargaining power to farmers, workers and consumers; and the redistribution of income toward "a middle-class standard of life."[6] This did not reduce his concern over the dangers of gradual collectivism and the related assumption that majorities expressed the will of society.

He was familiar with the writings of John Maynard Keynes with whom he had entered into correspondence in the 1930s.[7] He was also aware of the work of major contributors of the Austrian School. In correspondence with Professor Lionel C. Robbins, dated March 24, 1937, he indicated familiarity with the work of Friedrich A. von Hayek and Ludwig von Mises. He felt that Hayek and Mises did not "arrive at a positive theory of liberalism which gives a method of social control consistent with the exchange economy."[8]

Lippman turned to the rule of law which he considered a solution to many of the problems he had contemplated so long. "It checked the will of the majority. It guarded against the tyranny of the governor. It permitted established, informed, and accountable public agencies to shape the economy of the state." Lippman's brand of liberalism advocated that noble men search for a "higher" law to overcome the arbitrary acts of "their lords and masters . . . mobs at home and barbarians abroad, and the vagrant willfulness of their own spirits." "The denial that men may be arbitrary," argued Lippman, "is the higher law," a higher law particularly important in the period in which he wrote, one of the great periods of disorder.[9] In effect, a solution to society's problem is to be found in a conception of natural law.

Even as Lippman stressed the rule of law he put his faith in an elite of intelligence and character and counted himself among them. "A good citizen in a good society . . . ruled by 'his second and civilized nature,' not by his instincts . . . the noble master of his own weaker and meaner passions . . . mastery was the 'aristocratic code' . . . not inherent in prerogative and birth but functional to the capacity to rule."[10]

He also warned that the ideals of the good life and good society would fall far short of perfection. His observations of reality moved him to stress the necessity of protecting human freedom by constitutional means thereby holding government to a higher law.[11]

The good turn taken by human thought in the seventeenth and eighteenth centuries and the wrong turn in the middle of the nineteenth century is the source of the ongoing debate and search to which Lippman and many others contributed and with which this study as well is concerned.

The issues raised in the debate have become all the more important because the authority of the state since the mid–1930s has been enlarged presumably to provide social control. This expansion has been expedient but not glorious, necessary but dangerous, useful but costly. Along with this expansion has been renewed concern over the moral and social values underpinning the market. It would serve us well if we could avoid becoming "hopelessly entangled in the errors" of past generations.

We have no assurance that we will be spared such errors. Observers note, for instance, that prior to America's entry into World War I in 1917, the country had the most decentralized, dispersed, regionalized and localized government to be found among western nations. As a consequence of its entry into World War I, the country became a highly centralized, collectivized war state.

Following World War I and the dismantling of the "war" state, something strange happened. According to Robert Nisbet, Americans began to yearn for the sense of togetherness which radiated during the war from the government in Washington and which unified the nation as never before.[12] Heretofore recessive in manner and frugal in the use of its powers, the national government now forged ahead of states, local communities, professions, businesses, churches and other traditional sources of close solidarity. The legacy so promoted, according to Nisbet, was the intoxicating idea of "national community."

Slowly and inexorably the state took on roles once left to families, churches and local communities. Franklin Roosevelt's New Deal, the welfare state, the Great Society are but cases in point. Promoted and envisioned as a solution to the increased uncertainty brought about by the breakdown caused by the Great Depression, the breakdown itself was brought about in good measure by a collapse in national monetary and banking institutions ostensibly designed to promote a "national community" and to make the uncertain certain.[13] The concept of "national community" served to burden Americans with a vast and impersonal bureaucracy. At the same time America also increased its risk to the fatal diseases of empires in history: apoplexy at the center and anemia at the extremities.

To be sure, the idea of community as we have discussed is critical to the American Puritan concept of a "holy commonwealth," the classical principle of the "general good" and the Scottish ideal of "benevolence." It is not surprising that Americans looked to the idea of a national community as a means for reinforcing the country's ability to cope with the vagaries of future time.

Unlike many others in the "America-in-decline" set, Nisbet is more optimistic on America's economic, social, and political future. For one thing, he feels that there is growing evidence that America's worship of centralization and bureauracy has peaked. A national community for all its vaunted advantages has also brought with it unintended and less desired consequences of increased centralization and vast bureaucracy, including a wobbly central monetary authority.

Indeed, in other advanced industrial democracies, economic, political, and social trends are away from centralization. Much the same is true in countries that have not been working democracies in the past. All the more reason to take these trends seriously and not dismiss them either as an aberrant passion by an electorate momentarily seduced by state-sponsored consumerism, or as the deserved triumph of common sense patriots over the looney left and the wimpy center. Certainly socialism with its focus on redistribution, not on production, has become irrelevant to the faltering industrial states and even more so to the Soviet Union and its allies.

INDIVIDUALIST AND COLLECTIVIST CONFLICT

J. M. Keynes shared Lippmann's views regarding the need to turn the business of government to an enlightened and bureaucratic and political elite. Keynes was also aware of the eighteenth-century contribution to philosophic thought that human nature is reasonable, that man is a rational being. It was this rationalist belief that "underlay the ethics of self-interest . . . rational self-interest. . . . it was because self-interest was rational that the egoistic and altruistic systems were supposed to work out in practice to the same conclusion."[14] Yet in his philosophic insights, Keynes neglected his own central contribution to economics; that pursuit of individual self-interest will not ensure full employment, not prevent inflationary wage bargains.

Keynes also agreed with Lippmann that to tame the market and to manage the market explicit cooperation is required by individuals acting through the medium of the state. Both also shared the view that the task should be turned over to an enlightened bureaucratic and political elite. Both recognized the underlying morality of the market system, although Keynes managed to keep morality and economics in separate compartments. As a consequence Keynes simply skipped over the problem.[15]

What is to prevent the bureaucratic and governing political elite from maximizing their individual advantage? Keynes assumed as Lippmann that these people would be motivated by higher goals of maximization of their private interests and that standards of public behavior would progress in a way that gradually put less rather than more emphasis on maximizing monetary gain. Appeal to these higher motives enabled both Keynes and Lippmann to bypass the implementation problem of superimposing collective objectives on an individualistic calculus.[16] The problem with this approach, critics note, is that it obscures the individualist-collectivist conflict.[17]

Indeed, the issue of motivation of the bureaucratic and political elite turns out to be critical. It may well be that contemporary public policies operating without benefit of a supportive morality and explicit rules-oriented policy-constraints places additional strain on the market mechanism. The net effect will serve to undermine the foundations of the market mechanism itself.

The problem of enlightened paternalism is taken into explicit account by many monetarists in the Chicago tradition and in the development of market liberalism. The approach is to avoid the problem by making required changes in individual behavior through requirements of law and alterations in market opportunities. In effect, the idea is to constrain the activities of the bureaucratic and political elite in a rules-oriented policy system—

thus depriving their exercise of discretionary powers. This approach also side steps the issue of morality. The individual, as one critic put it, "is invited to choose the morality as well as the God of his own choice."[18]

For Keynes the received doctrines of the nineteenth century served, as we have discussed, as a point of departure for the shaping of a managed market economy. We have noted that he opposed extreme *laissez-faire* for the most part by a pragmatic, empirical, and counter-philosophical approach. To his critics, he was seen as opening the way for collectivism by way of careless pragmatism and a misguided belief in the capacity of the political-legislative processes to improve social welfare.

Of course, Keynes for his part held in disdain both politicians and the opinions of the general public. And, indeed, he shared the view common to England's elite that while *laissez-faire* may well have been the philosophy in office, the governing philosophy was basically very pragmatic. Its very strength lay in its nonideological capability.[19] For many of the liberal elite, Keynesianism was seen as having the same characteristics. It was a middle way—an apolitical alternative to the polarized political choice of the time. At the same time, pragmatic, anti-ideological Keynesianism provided the political and administrative elite a means for satisfying itself and the electorate of its legitimacy and its policies. Given that the political and administrative elite was morally, intellectually, and otherwise superior to individual businessmen, the ruling bureaucracy's position was secure.

Basically, the idea of managed capitalism was for the state to establish appropriate "rules of the game" and manipulate the market and law so as to alter the market choices facing individuals. For their part, such social organizations as unions were expected to show restraint in their activities. Together these elements provided society with a framework within which individuals would be free to pursue their own objectives. The fact is, however, that the more state intervention is resorted to the more its operation depends on individualistic calculus in some of its important sectors and on the virtues and moral standards of both the ruling bureaucratic elite and the populace. The most important are truth, honesty, physical restraint, and respect for law.

It has been underscored that standards of behavior are very

important for decentralized economies. This is also true for centrally guided economies. In centrally guided economies, regulation will be very costly if behavior responds only to individual advantage and if the bureaucratic elite attempts to push its controls solely on the basis of private self-interest. By whom will the performance indicators be set?

The analogy of the use of a price mechanism by central authorities and the independent operation of such a mechanism is of only limited value. It is important to harness market prices with individual incentives. Market prices will simply not carry out their signalling function efficiently if they are open to manipulation by central authorities or others.

The problem faced by the central authorities in a system of managed capitalism is essentially how to hold individual preference and maximization to its social purpose. There is no easy way to communicate to an individual and a business when maximization of private interests is to stop and when to consider national interests. Thus, individuals are to seek the maximum reward for their services, but individuals organized in unions are to exercise restraint. Business is to maximize profits but not at the expense of national interests. Where is the line to be drawn and by whom? We have discussed earlier a way out of the difficulty through a rules-oriented policy system. The provisions of statutory rules and incentives along the lines suggested by Milton Friedman and others would permit private parties to operate according to their own incentives within the framework of statutory rules.

Critics point out that in practice reliance on such inducements must be accompanied by supported adaptations in individual norms of behavior if regulation is to be effective. Otherwise, the authorities are simply "unable to diagnose, implement, and enforce the intended correctives to individual behavior in response to the norm of private maximization in the underlying market situation. . . . A purely individualistic ethic will therefore weaken or impede the efficiency of these correctives themselves."[20]

For these reasons, among others, critics argue that the extension of state intervention in the market economy increases the need for a link between motives that operate on the individual level and the desired outcome for society. Individuals can be expected to cooperate and meet the needs of society only if they feel this to be their own interest, duty, or social obligation. The decline of traditional ties has only made the situation worse. And, according to some critics, the only remaining basis for social obligation has become civic duty to uphold a just society.

In fact, "acceptance of the market economy as a just one thereby becomes a condition of its stability . . . macromorality of the system thereby becomes integrally connected with what is required for it to function smoothly. . . . This works a major change . . . justification for managed capitalism has always been a pragmatic one, residing in overall results of the system, has been precisely its presumed ability to do without ethical judgements and moral obligations based upon them."[21]

Our discussion has suggested Keynes' views on the macromorality of capitalism. Simply put, he viewed managed capitalism as the unattractive system with the least bad results.[22] For Keynes it is better that an individual occupy himself making money rather than being a political lord over his contemporaries. In his judgment, economic objectives had their place for another generation or so. Unlike Bentham and Marx, Keynes felt that too much should not be made of the economic dimension of human life.

Fred Hirsch makes the point that "the Keynesian contribution can now be seen as representing the high water mark of secular liberalism, attempting the ultimate in privatization—the addition of morality to the sphere of individual choice, yet . . . the crucial social underpinnings of the market process are themselves weakened by the full permeation of an individualistic calculus."[23]

The shortcomings of such an approach were for the most part covered up by the English tradition of enlightened paternalism. Hirsch goes on to conclude that this "paternalist cover has been removed in the formulation of market liberalism that has been developed most thoroughly in the modern Chicago tradition" [e.g., Milton Friedman, *Capitalism and Freedom* (Chicago: University of Chicago Press, 1962)].[24]

The issue is that in Keynes' view of managed capitalism, the paternalist cover does play a significant role, according to Hirsch, "precisely because of its unquestioning reliance on obligations and instincts deriving from an earlier preindustrial culture . . . in the complete Keynesian system that we can best observe the limits of the guided market, because Keynes took for granted supportive characteristics that his own system could not preserve but that the purer system of his successors in economic liberalism ignored."[25]

In taking for granted these supportive characteristics of earlier systems, Keynes side stepped the moral issue underpinning his own system. But in so doing, an unintended consequence was to undermine the very foundations on which rested the market system he sought to preserve. Without the benefit of the English paternalist cover, there is indeed good reason to question the inclination and capacity of a bureaucratic and political elite operating within undefined policy systems to serve the national rather than its own interest.

NOTES

1. Walter Lippman, "Letter to William Allen White, June 28, 1937," in John Morton Blum, ed., *Public Philosophies Selected Letters of Walter Lippman* (New York: Ticknor and Fields, 1985): p. 362; Walter Lippman, *Good Society* (New York: Grosset and Dunlap, 1943, first published in 1937).

2. Lippman, *Good Society*: pp. 46–7 also quoted in Blum, *Public Philosophies*: p. xxxii.

3. Ibid., p. xxxii.

4. Ibid.

5. Quoted in Blum, *Public Philosophies*: pp. xxxii–xxxiii.

6. Ibid., p. xxxiii.

7. The relevant correspondence Lippmann to Keynes April 17, 1934 (ibid., p. 317); January 9, 1935 (ibid., 322); January 31, 1940 (ibid., p. 386); April 2, 1942 (ibid., pp. 419–421); March 23, 1945 (ibid., p. 463); January 2, 1946 (ibid., p. 478).

8. Ibid., p. 357.

9. Ibid., pp. xxxiii–xxxiv.

10. Ibid., p. xlvi.

11. Ibid., p. xlvii.

12. See the interview given by Robert Nisbet in R. M. Kidder, "Nation as Community: A Mixed Blessing for U.S.," *The Christian Science Monitor* (May 26, 1988): pp. 19–20.

13. See the classic study Milton Friedman and Anna J. Schwartz, *A Monetary History of the United States 1867–1960* (Princeton: Princeton University Press, 1963).

14. J. M. Keynes, "My Early Beliefs," *Collected Writings* (London: St. Martin, 1971–73), vol. X: p. 446.

15. Fred Hirsch, *Social Limits to Growth* (Cambridge: Harvard University Press, 1977 Second Printing): p. 134.

16. Hirsch points out that in the American liberal tradition, which leans less on enlightened paternalism, there is a chance for greater conflict. Ibid., p. 124.

17. Ibid.

18. Ibid., p. 138.

19. Hirsch, *Social Limits to Growth*: p. 126.

20. Ibid., p. 132.

21. Ibid., pp. 132–133.

22. Ibid., p. 134.

23. Ibid., p. 122.

24. Ibid.

25. Ibid.

Chapter 7

State Money

MONEY AND THE COMMUNITY

It seems particularly unusual in the on-going debate between Keynesians, monetarists, and Austrians that some of the participants forget that Keynes shares with them a common monetary heritage. In good measure the misunderstanding stems from Keynes' preference for discretionary monetary policy exercised by an enlightened elite as we have noted.

His preference, in part, can be rationalized by appeal to monetary nominalism, chartalism or better state money. To begin with, Keynes writes that the "money-of-account" is the primary concept of the theory of money.[1] In effect, money proper can exist only in relation to a "money-of-account."[2] He argues that money-of-account is the description or title and "money" is the thing which answers to the description.[3] If the same thing is always answered, writes Keynes, to the same description the distinction would have no practical interest.[4] On the other hand, if the thing that is called money can change while its description remains the same, the distinction can indeed be significant.[5]

As for contracts and promises to deliver goods and services in the future, custom or law serve as the basis for their enforcement according to Keynes. At this point, the state or community is introduced, for it is they which enforce delivery, "but also which decides what it is that must be delivered as lawful or customary discharge of a contract which has been concluded in terms of money-of-account."[6] The state, therefore, comes in first of all as the authority of law which enforces the payment of the thing which corresponds to the name or description in the contract. But it comes in doubly when, in addition, "it claims the right to determine and declare *what thing* corresponds to the name, and to vary its declaration from time to time—when, it claims the right to re-edit the dictionary. This right is claimed by all modern states and has been so claimed by some four thousand years at least. It is when this stage in the evolution of money has been reached that Knapp's chartalism—the doctrine that money is peculiarly a creation of the state—is fully realized."[7]

In Keynes' view, all money is chartalist or state money. Bank money, for its part, is simply an acknowledgment of private debt expressed in the money-of-account used alongside or alternatively with money-paper to settle a transaction. He includes in the *Treatise on Money* as state-money, not only that which is compulsory legal-tender but also money which the state or the Central Bank undertakes to accept in payments to itself or to exchange for compulsory legal-tender money.[8]

Managed money, according to Keynes, is the most generalized form of money. This type of money can be "considered to degenerate with commodity money on the one side when the managing authority holds against it a hundred percent of the objective standard, so that it is in effect a warehouse warrant, and into fiat money on the other side when it loses its objective standard."[9] Keynes argues "chartalism begins when the state *designates* the objective standard which shall correspond to the money-of-account. Representative money begins when money is no longer composed of its objective standard. Fiat money only appears when the state goes a step further and abandons the objective standard, coined money, which the state alone can mint and which may have a value superior to that of the commodity of which it is composed, is at the most a first step in the direction of representative money."[10]

INTRINSIC VALUE OF MONEY

The concept of the intrinsic value of money considered important by gold standard supporters including Simmel and the Austrians receives little support from Keynes. In his view, these people with their emphasis on the intrinsic value of money are pursuing a "mirage" or a "will-o'-the-wisp." It is better, he argues, to substitute for the notion of the value of money the notion of general purchasing power of money.

This substitution implies a very different pattern of thought which, in turn, entails a different way of conducting monetary policy. The purchasing power of money is viewed as depending upon the price level of the goods and services on which money income is expended. The concept implies a certain cause-and-effect relationship. The purchasing power of money is high if prices are low and vice versa. The monetary authorities for their part working under this concept aim at stabilizing the purchasing power of money by influencing the general level of prices for goods and services including wages.

If the monetary authorities, on the other hand, are operating under the concept of the value of money, they have no choice but to stabilize the value of money. Under these circumstances, the value of money is the "cause," and the price level is the "effect." A commodity standard such as the gold standard makes such a task easier. Thus, the value of money (i.e., dollar, pound, franc, dinar, etc.), is defined in terms of the commodity (e.g., gold). The job of the authorities is to keep the currency convertible into, say gold, the commodity at the official price. In effect, instead of concerning itself with the general price level, the authority is concerned with only one price which is the value of money.

This is the relationship under the gold standard which advocates such in its support. For a contractual society, argue gold standard advocates, free convertibility into gold is a principal plank upon which such a society rests. Diminish the importance of the value of money concept, and you undermine the base on which a contractual society rests. They argue that Keynes' concept of the general purchasing power lends itself to state manipulation of money, including permanent manipulation called inflation.

In fact, Keynes' detractors argue first—thanks to his *Treatise on Money*—an opposite view of money gained currency whose ultimate consequence since the Bretton-Woods Agreement has been to sever nearly all links between gold and money.[11] The Jamaica Agreement, put into effect in 1978, substituted "Special Drawing Rights," a form of monetary asset issued by the International Monetary Fund (IMF), for gold as a unit of account. This paper unit presumably now serves as the reference point for the world monetary system.

To its critics, one problem with state money is that a debtor (in particular the state or government) could claim to discharge a debt by merely declaring what should be regarded as discharging it. The idea that a debt can be discharged by "declaration" that it has been paid is simply so much double talk and as such unacceptable to these critics. It suggests that a debt can be kept outstanding by an infinite number of promises to pay at some unspecified date. Voluntary acceptance of such debt is not fulfillment of a contract but the making of a new one. If such an arrangement is brought about by compulsion, "we are brought back to the position that the debt has not been borrowed. I assert that the idea that the state, can as of right, abrogate debts in this way by 'declaring' them to be 'money' fails to take into account the moral context in terms of which, in a free society, they arise."[12]

Frankel goes on to argue that Keynes' claim that all "civilised money" is chartalist and a "creation of the state" really places "discussion of the nature, meaning, and significance of money outside moral discourse and beyond the moral structure of a free community. A possible reason for the claim is because Keynes fails to make one adequate distinction between the power of the state and the institutional evolution of society: between the role of government and the role of custom. I am not deterred from this view by the fact that at times he appears to use the terms of state and community interchangeably."[13]

What is distressing to such critics as Frankel is that Keynes' frequent appeals to morality draw from his definitions of money on the highly legalistic views of Georg Fredrich Knapp. It is Knapp's argument that money is created and regulated by the state. The value of money *per se* is secondary. It serves previously to discharge debt which is a power given to money by the state. Such a definition of money is not based on any particular moral conception. It is formal, judicial, and historical. And it is, in Frankel's view, a concept of money which is "fallacious and that has had and continues to have a very deleterious influence on monetary thought and policy."[14]

In its ultimate sophistication, the state's monetary role is simply the creation of new purchasing power out of nothing.[15] The fact is, however, that nothing can be created out of nothing. Ultimately such efforts at money creation rest on trust and the belief that the borrower will indeed create something with which he will be able to repay the lender. With all due respect to those writers who stress the positive benefits of the increasing sophistication of monetary and financial arrangements for the economy, attempts by monetary authorities to actively create credit with the knowledge that such creation will lead to a debasement of money will only succeed in promoting mistrust and uncertainty.

In the final analysis, monetary institutions and the state cannot "create at will" the goods and services which money will purchase. The simple granting of claims by such authorities is one thing; what such claims will indeed purchase depends on society's ability and willingness to produce and fulfill such claims. The granting of wage claims, for instance, is one thing. What these wages will indeed purchase is something else again. Frankel puts it well when he argues that when "creation" of money ceases to be related to its social and economic circumstances, the "will" of the state cannot prevent its currency from losing domestic and international value. Even granting that the state may be able to enforce by decree its "will" domestically, chances for international acceptance of such a currency arrangement are remote indeed. In the view of Frankel and others, "there should be as little difference as possible between what men said or promised about money and what it was seen to be by all who had to make use of it to express their rights, promises, and obligations."[16]

These critics argue that current arrangements really amount to the notes of such central banks as the Federal Reserve System really being promises to pay itself. That is to say, we have, in effect, "IOU nothing" money. We have had IOU money in the past. Such examples as the *assignats* of the French Revolution, the Continental dollar, and the Civil War greenback. The proper course, they argue, is to re-monetize gold. In their view, money is not chosen by governments. It is chosen by the market. People do not consider paper money in the abstract. They think of it as a standard of value.

A prominent American political figure, former Congressman Jack Kemp (Republican, New York), puts forth the case for gold:

> We need gold convertibility because it's not enough simply to have a rule for monetary policy; there must also be a mechanism for putting it into

effect. The most stable monetary mechanism we have seen was the classical gold standard. Its record in this country might have been even better if not for the shortcomings of the banking system before there was a Federal Reserve. And the Bretton-Woods system, though flawed, provided exceptional stability.[17]

He chides his former colleague, Congressman Henry Reuss, who predicted in 1968 that if gold convertibility were suspended, "the price of gold would fall from $35 to $6 an ounce. Instead, the price is now above $300 and has been as high as $850."[18]

Congressman Kemp and others of similar persuasion believe that gold has no politics. Gold requires no elaborate system of controls. It is international. It is stable. It is just. It does not take from the weak and give to the strong.

Keynes, on the other hand, had other ideas regarding the gold standard. Thus he writes in 1924:

In truth, the gold standard is already a barbaric relic. All of us, from the Governor of the Bank of England downwards, are now primarily interested in preserving the stability of business, prices, and employment and are not likely, when the choice is forced on us, deliberately to sacrifice these to outworn dogma. . . . Advocates of the ancient standard do not observe how remote it is now from the spirit and requirement of the age. A regulated non-metallic standard has slipped in unnoticed. *It exists*. Whilst economists dozed, the academic dream of a hundred years, doffing its cap and gown, clad in paper rags has crept into the real world by means of the God fairies—always so much more potent than the good—the wicked ministers of Finance.[19]

He goes on to argue that even the more enlightened advocates of the gold standard "do not welcome it as the return of a 'natural' currency and instead, quite decidedly, that it shall be a 'managed' one. They allow gold back only as a constitutional monarch, shorn of his ancient despotic powers and compelled to accept the advice of a Parliament of Banks."[20]

Moreover, Keynes particularly stressed that gold does indeed come with political baggage. Thus, he argued that Britain's return to gold would mean surrender of its monetary policy to the American Federal Reserve Board. The preponderance of power would shift from the Bank of England to the Board to the disadvantage of Great Britain.[21]

He explicitly rejects a return to gold along pre-World War I lines as well as any "managed" gold standard in cooperation with the United States. Such an arrangement he argues "retains too many of the disadvantages of the old system without its advantages, and because it would make us too dependent on the policy and on the wishes of the Federal Reserve Board."[22]

The application of the same policy, argues Keynes, is not necessarily always in the interests of both countries. He regards the stability of prices, credit, and employment as the goals of economic policy. The gold standard whether "managed" or otherwise is simply incapable of serving these goals according to Keynes.

I have discussed elsewhere the issue of a "return to gold."[23] A summary of the observations is appropriate here given the tendency on the part of some gold advocates to idealize the gold standard and to overlook some of its more troublesome aspects. Thus, between 1815 and 1914, there were twelve major crises or panics in the United States which pushed up interest rates, created severe unemployment, and suspended specie payments (conversion of the dollar into gold) in addition to 14 more minor recessions.[24] To be sure, between 1879 and 1965—a period when America was on some sort of gold standard (the dollar's fiscal links with gold were not cut until 1971 during President Nixon's administration)—the consumer price index rose by an average of 1.4 percent a year. On the other hand, the same bouts of inflation were followed by deep deflation, in which prices actually fell. For instance, in 1921's world recession, when production actually fell for only a few months, there were 30–40 percent cuts in manufacturing wages in some countries in the period 1920–1922.

Experience with the gold standard has not prevented attempts to have gold serve in some capacity in the monetary system. American former Secretary of Treasury, James A. Baker, suggested in 1987, gold's restoration as a guidepost for the world monetary system.[25] His proposal calls for an inflation index based on gold and commodity prices. Coupled with measures of growth, employment, and trade, the commodities index would help the leading industrial countries bring their economies into harmony and their currencies into stability.

Baker's gold proposal, however, is viewed as compromising the economic sovereignty of a country as Keynes observed earlier regarding a similar proposal based on gold. Thus, Karl Otto Pohl, President of the German Bundesbank, protests that "no government and no central bank can accept a quasi-automatic mechanism," such as a commodity index, to set policies.[26] Others simply wondered if gold were not already a forgotten question. In any case, a managed system will indeed need some sort of anchor once if, in fact, floating exchange rates are to be abandoned.

What is often lacking with various proposals for some sort of gold standard is an appreciation and understanding of the fact that the gold standard was more than a monetary standard. It cannot be understood, as it cannot be operated successfully, except as part of a socioeconomic political and philosophic system in which it was operated. This system no longer exists.

The contemporary world differs radically from that of the early nineteenth century whose revolutions were aimed at assuring political and economic liberty by breaking through the outworn controls of a preceding age of regulations. For the most part, the revolutions of our time have been protests against the philosophy and institutions of the system of individualism based on natural rights. They aimed at the opposite values of social control, and they have created myths and utopias which differ radically from the nineteenth century utopias of individual liberty. The impersonal forces of the market in which classical (and neo-classical) economists relied to bring about a maximal production and distribution of income which, if not equitable, would at least be effective in maintaining high production, tend now to be displaced as political ideals by such objectives as full employment and various social safety net programs.

Inevitably these objectives imply intervention and regulation. And the only mechanisms presently available for such intervention and regulation are those of the nation state. The evidence for this is to be found on every hand, and nowhere is it more conclusive than in the field of domestic and international monetary affairs. Monetary policies directed toward various goals including stabilizing the national income constitute a formidable reinforcement of nationalism in the economic sphere. Whatever may be thought of the wisdom or practicality of such intervention, the fact must be recognized that the nineteenth century integration of market processes has been impaired by the emergence in every country of a greater measure of state intervention particularly in monetary affairs.

Keynes and his ideas, together with his followers, provided much to the intellectual leadership for the changed world environment. Already in the closing years of the first post-World War I decades, Keynes was edging from the *Tract in Monetary Reform* and the *Treatise* towards the *General Theory* and to more wide ranging world problems. His vision of the world, however, already stands out in his *The Economic Consequences of the Peace* (London: Macmillan, 1919).

Joseph A. Schumpeter puts it succinctly when he writes that in the "Economic Consequences of the Peace, we find nothing of the theoretical apparatus of the 'General Theory.' But we find the whole of the vision of things social and economic of which that apparatus is the technical complement. The 'General Theory' is the final result of a long struggle to make that vision of our age analytically operative."[27]

Schumpeter adds that we have here "the origin of the modern stagnation thesis. . . . Every comprehensive 'theory' . . . of an economic state of society consists of two complementary but essentially distinct elements. There is first, the theorist's view about the basic features of that state of society, about what is and what is not important in order to understand its life at a given time. Let us call this his vision. And there is, second, the theorist's technique, an apparatus by which he conceptualizes his vision and which turns the latter into concrete propositions of 'theories.' "[28]

Keynes, moreover, had little doubt in the intellectual leadership and in the wisdom of a chosen few who would serve to make the necessary judgments on such critical issues as how much the community as a whole would save and invest. To Keynes, the central problem was individual choice in the face of uncertainty. The solution was to be found in part by the deliberate and direct control of money and credit by a central institution and in part by the dissemination of information on as wide a scale as possible. Despair over uncertainty and lack of information by the public pushed Keynes to favor a so-called "directive intelligence" as a means for dealing with these issues. This, in turn, translated into government intervention into economic affairs and indirect control and manipulation of the monetary and financial organization. Thus, there is no room for anything but a "managed monetary standard."

NOTES

1. J. M. Keynes, *A Treatise on Money*, Vol. I (London: Macmillan, 1930): p. 3.
2. Ibid.
3. Ibid., pp. 3–4.
4. Ibid., p. 4.
5. Thus, Keynes writes, "The difference is like that between the King of England (whoever it may be) and King George. A contract to pay ten years hence a weight of gold equal to the weight of the King of England is not the same thing as a contract to pay a weight of gold equal to the weight of the individual who is now King George. It is for the State to declare when the time comes, who the King of England is." Ibid., p. 4.
6. Ibid.
7. Ibid.
8. Ibid., p. 6.
9. Ibid., p. 8.
10. Ibid., p. 9.
11. See Paul Fabra, "Keynes and the Modern Debasement of Money," *Wall Street Journal* (March 30, 1982): p. 32.
12. S. Herbert Frankel, *Two Philosophies of Money: The Conflict of Trust and Authority* (New York: St. Martin's Press, 1978): p. 46.
13. Ibid., pp. 47–8.
14. Ibid., p. 48.
15. Ibid., p. 49. For this observation, Frankel draws on J. A. Schumpeter, *The Theory of Economic Development* (Oxford: Oxford University Press, 1961): p. 73.
16. Frankel, *Two Philosophies of Money*: p. 56. He puts the point at issue succinctly by quoting an old African proverb: "I cannot hear what you are saying because I see what you are."
17. Jack Kemp, "The Renewal of Western Monetary Standards," *Wall Street Journal* (April 7, 1982): p. 30.
18. Ibid.
19. J. M. Keynes, *Monetary Reform* (New York: Harcourt, Brace, and Company, 1924): p. 187. Italics in original.
20. Ibid.
21. Ibid., pp. 187–89.
22. Ibid., pp. 190–91.

23. George Macesich, *The Politics of Monetarism: Its Historical and Institutional Development* (Totowa, NJ: Rowman and Allanheld, 1984): pp. 10–12.

24. *The Economist* (September 19, 1981): pp. 17–8.

25. "Baker's Plan: No Glitter," *Business Week* (October 19, 1987): p. 56.

26. Ibid.

27. Joseph A. Schumpeter in *The New Economics*, Seymour Harris, ed. (New York: Alfred A. Knopf, 1947): p. 80. Quote by S. Herbert Frankel, *Two Philosophies of Money*: pp. 63–4.

28. Ibid., p. 127 n. 22.

Chapter 8

In Search of a Monetary Standard

KEYNES' EFFORTS

As a monetary economist, Keynes was looking for a monetary standard which could be workable. In the *Treatise on Money* (1930), he was critical of the restored gold standard in the post-World War I era. His criticism was directed toward attempts to make the gold standard work as it had been re-instituted. He was, however, seeking to make it work.[1] By the 1930s and into World War II, he was still searching for a reformed monetary standard that would be workable as we know from his work in the creation of the International Monetary Fund.

Where in relation to Keynes' search for a reformed monetary standard stands his *General Theory* of 1936? Certainly the years when the book was being written were years of monetary upheaval. The monetary crisis was indeed due to an inadequacy in the supply of base money, consisting of gold, as many economists during and since the crisis have argued. This is certainly consistent with what Keynes was to call a rise in liquidity preference. In effect, there was not enough base money for the banking system to be able to come to the rescue. Subsequent devaluations of the pound sterling and dollar in 1931 and 1933, respectively, removed the monetary constraint against expansion as John Hicks argues.

How far would be safe to allow such an expansion to go? This was the point, argues Hicks "where the revolution in Keynes' own thinking occurred. It was here that he had to pass from consideration of the monetary system (the understanding of which he was a master) to consideration of the real economy, which I fear must be recognized that he understood it less well. It is true that long before he wrote the *General Theory*, he had been turning that way. His *Treatise* (1930) had been narrowly money; it was concerned with price levels and with their variations, not with output and employment. But even before he finished the *Treatise*, he was claiming he knew how to 'conquer unemployment.' That the prescription he was offering in his 1928 pamphlets would have involved a devaluation of sterling is, one may be sure, a consequence he would not have refused."[2]

Keynes was, of course, aware that focusing on employment could be a dangerous target. Given the need between 1928 to 1935 "to conquer unemployment," he was quite willing to do so. He defined "full employment" as the maximum that could be reached by expansionary measures even though some residue of unemployment would still be out of reach to such measures. Hicks calls unemployment curable along the lines suggested by Keynes as "Keynesian unemployment."

In working out his theory, Keynes was assisted by assuming that the level of money wages is in practice rather rigid. This was not an assumption which he accepted only for the benefit of the General Theory. It is, in fact, a belief that goes back at least to 1925 and his attack on the British return to the gold standard of the old parity. And indeed, Hicks writes, "it was in relation to the then existing level of money wages that he was claiming that sterling, after April 1925 was overvalued. It is doubtless true that during the 1920s and 1930s, the wage level in Britain was becoming more 'sticky' in money terms. But when one considers the great variations, both upward and downward that had occurred in 1918–1921, to have laid such stress upon rigidity, when rigidity had set in so recently, does seem peculiar."[3]

The tasks for economists and economics become much easier if we assume that wages are not only constant but rigid. It must be supposed that in the conditions of "Keynesian unemployment" that the wage level, as Hicks points out, must be rigid so it is unaffected by changes in other variables. Thus, it is, argues Hicks, "the Keynes model is not just formally expressed in wage units; it is on a labour standard. . . . A labour standard expresses the value of money in terms of labour, just as the gold standard expressed it in terms of gold."[4]

Under the gold standard, central banks stood ready to exchange money for gold as long as their gold reserves lasted. Under normal conditions and with care, such conversions could continue without endangering the standard. The trouble with the labor standard, of course, is that it has no reserves. There is no bank, no authority which can guarantee the convertibility of money and labor. It is for this reason, argues Hicks, that it is only a pseudo-standard. For it is the labor standard that is the "major weakness of the Keynes theory and of the policies that had been based on it."[5]

If indeed the monetary system adjusts itself to the level of money wages as envisioned in the *General Theory*, then sociopolitical forces gain in power relative to the economic forces. Among these forces are included, of course, labor unions. Others, as Hicks underscores, include the behavior of prices of the goods on which wages are spent. Since it is real wages in which labor unions and their members are interested, we have the making of a vicious circle of rising prices and wages all too familiar in the post-war period. In addition, we have no anchor for the long-term price level.

A THEORETICAL FRAMEWORK

The issues involved can be illustrated by drawing on a theoretical framework set forth by Milton Friedman in "A Theoretical Framework for Monetary Analysis" which is also one that most economists, including monetarists and Keynesians, would accept.[6] It is ideologically neutral and thus useful in analyzing fluctuations in income and prices in a wide variety of institutional and sociopolitical arrangements.

Assuming a closed economy and neglecting the fiscal role of government, Friedman's framework, cast into a basic IS-LM apparatus, can be described as follows:

$$C/P = f(Y/P, r) \quad (1)$$

$$I/P = g[i] \quad (2)$$

$$Y/P = C/P + I/P \quad (3)$$

$$M_d = P_1(P/Y, r) \quad (4)$$

$$M_s = h[i] \quad (5)$$

$$M_d = M_s \quad (6)$$

Where: C = Consumption
P = Price Level
Y = Income
r = Interest Rate
M_d = Demand for Money
M_s = Supply of Money

Friedman does not consider in dispute the demand-for-money equation, which is here written in a general version acceptable to most economists. At issue is the method of completing the system that has seven variables but only six equations in it. According to Friedman, the choice is either

$$P = P_o \tag{7}$$

which is the Keynesian income expenditure theory or

$$Y/P = y = y_o \tag{8}$$

as in the quantity theory of money. Equation (7) represents the case of rigid prices. In this instance, the price level is determined outside the system, which again reduces the system to one of six equations in six unknowns. It assumes that prices are set or administered by the bargaining power of respective parties such as unions, oligopolies, and other institutional arrangements that restrict price flexibility. Views attributing inflation to one or another variety of cost-push causes are a manifestation of equation (7).

A number of cost-push and administered price inflation theories are discussed in the literature.[7] I call these theories anti-traditionalist or cost-pusher views. As discussed in the literature, Phillips curve contributions represent attempts, for the most part, to link real magnitudes and the rate of change in prices to their initial historically determined level.

Equation (8) is a statement that the economy is operational at the full employment level of real income. That is, real income is determined outside the system by appending the Walrasian equations of general equilibrium to it and regarding them as independent of equations defining the aggregates. Again, the system is reduced to one of six equations determining six unknowns. Friedman notes that this is the essence of the so-called classical dichotomy. In effect, the division between consumption and investment and the "real" interest rate is also determined in a Walrasian "real" system, one that admits of growth. It is for this reason that quantity theorists and monetarists tend to concentrate on equations (4), (5), and (6). In their view, equations (1), (2), and (3) are a summarization of aggregation or subset of the Walrasian system.

This suggests one reason why quantity theorists and monetarists focus on increases in aggregate demand and specifically on increases in the stock of money as primary causes of inflation. These theories are known in the literature as "traditionalist" or "demand-pull" theories. Since changes in aggregate demand can be engineered also by fiscal policy manipulation, some advocates of demand-pull inflation may not share the monetarist conviction on the important role of the stock of money.

Following Friedman, for the simple quantity theory of money given that $Y/P = Y_o$, equations (1), (2), and (3) become a self-sustained set of three equations in three unknowns: C/P, I/P, and r.

Substituting (1) and (2) into (3), we have

$$Y_o - f(Y_o, r) = g(r), \qquad (9)$$

or a single equation that determines r. If we let r_o be this value of r, from equation (5), this determines the value of M, say M_o, which, using equation (6) converts (4) into

$$M_o = P_1(Y_o, r_o) \qquad (10)$$

which now determines P.

Equation (10), however, is simply the classical quantity theory of money equation. This may be seen by multiplying and dividing the right-hand side by Y_o and replacing 1 $(Y_o, r_o)/Y_o$ by V, which is its equivalent. Thus,

$$M_o = Py/V \qquad (11)$$

$$P = M_oV/Y \qquad (12)$$

For the Keynesian income expenditure theory, setting $P = P_o$ does not in general permit a sequential solution. The manner in which it is established is discussed above. By substituting equations (1) and (2) into (3), we have

$$Y/P_o - f(Y/P_o, r) = g(r) \tag{13}$$

one equation in two variables, Y and r. This is in fact Hicks' IS Curve of his IS-LM analysis. By substituting (4) and (5) into (6), we have

$$h(r) = P_o l(Y/P_o, r) \tag{14}$$

a second equation in the same two variables, Y and r. It is Hicks' LM Curve. The simultaneous solution of the two determines Y and r.

In keeping with the discussion, our simplified model (which Friedman points to as being faithful to Keynes) can be obtained by supposing that Y/P is not an argument in the right-hand side of equation (4) or that of absolute liquidity preference holds so that equation (4) takes the special form:

$$\begin{aligned} M_d &= 0 \text{ if } r > r_o \\ M_d &= \text{if } r < r_o \end{aligned} \tag{4a}$$

In these cases, equations (4), (5), and (6) determine the interest rate, $r = r_o$, as in the simple quantity theory of money equations (1), (2), and (3) do. Substituting the interest rate in equation (2) gives us investment, say of $I = I_o$, and in equation (1) makes consumption simply a function of income; so that real income must be determined by the requirement that it equate saving with investment.

Moving along with Friedman, if we approximate the function $f(Y/P, r_o)$ by a linear form—say,

$$C/P = C_o + C_1 Y/P \tag{15}$$

and substitute in equation (3) and solve for Y/P, we have

$$Y/P = C_o + I_o / 1 - C_1 \qquad (16)$$

which is the single Keynesian multiplier equation with $C_o + I_o$ equaling expenditure and $1/1 - C$ equaling the multiplier.

The key differences between the Keynesian view and monetarist view are that: Keynesians argue that change in the quantity of money affects spending via interest rate effect or spending; and the monetarist view underscores wealth in portfolios and then on final spending.

Neither the quantity theory nor the income-expenditure theory model is satisfactory as a framework for short-run analysis. According to Friedman, this is so mainly because neither theory can explain

> (a) the short-run division of a change in nominal income between prices and output, (b) the short-run adjustment of nominal income to change in autonomous variables, and (c) the transition between the short-run situation and a long-run equilibrium described essentially by the quantity theory model.[8]

A third way to determine the above system of equations is provided by Friedman in the monetary theory of nominal income.[9] This method draws on Irving Fisher's ideas on the nominal and real interest rates and Keynes' view that the current long-term market rate of interest is expected to prevail over a long period. The Keynes and Fisher synthesis is then integrated into a quantity theory model, together with the empirical assumptions that the real income elasticity of demand for money is unity, and that the difference between the anticipated real interest rate and the anticipated growth of real income is determined outside the system. In effect, this is the counterpart assumption to equations (7) and (8) of income expenditure and quantity theory, respectively. The result is a monetary model in which current income is related to current and prior quantities of money.[10] This monetary model of nominal income, according to Friedman, corresponds to the broader framework implicit in much of the theoretical and empirical work that he and others have done in analyzing monetary experience in the short run and is consistent with many of the empirical findings produced in these studies.

The quantity theory of money is basically a theory of the demand for money. It is at its best when the demand for money is a stable function of a few key variables. For instance, its stability is important because it ensures that, *mutatis mutandis*, inflationary pressures from a change in the supply of money are transmitted to the general level of prices.

DEMAND FOR MONEY

In the neoclassical analysis, the demand for money is functionally related to income, interest rates, and some types of wealth. The question of the nature of the income in the money demand function is still under debate: the current nominal income, real income, or Friedman's permanent income. The nature of the interest rate also commands attention: the short-term government bond rate, or the money market rate on private debt. In effect, the arguments or variables that enter the demand function for money, and the definition of the quantity of money appropriate for the demand function, have received substantial attention in both the recent and distant past. A number of studies seem to suggest that in the long run the demand for money function may not be stable. To judge from some of these studies, the function shifts over different phases of the cycle; no unique and stable function would therefore be obtained.[11] Money is one of the forms in which individuals can hold their assets. In some economies a small interest income is to be had from assets that are also used as money. But the desire to hold cash cannot be explained by this fact; there are many instances of money yielding no interest and being held nevertheless. Two peculiar and interrelated characteristics of money have usually been emphasized in theories that set it apart from other assets. The first is that money is acceptable as a means of exchange for goods and services, and the second is that its market value is generally highly predictable. These two characteristics are not the exclusive property of money. Other assets also possess them in varying degrees. However, unlike other assets, money is universally accepted as a means of exchange, and its value is usually more predictable than that of other assets. The three motives introduced by Keynes are the transactions, the precautionary, and the speculative motives. Keynes said, in developing in detail the motives of liquidity preference, that the subject was "substantially the same as that which has been sometimes discussed under the heading of the Demand for Money":

> It [the analysis of the motives to liquidity preference] is also closely connected with what is called the income-velocity of money—for the income-velocity of money merely measures what proportion of their incomes the public chooses to hold in cash, so that an increased income-velocity of money may be a symptom of a decreased liquidity preference. It is not the same thing [as the analysis of the motives to liquidity preference], however, since it is in respect to his stock of accumulated savings rather than his income, that the individual can exercise the choice between liquidity and illiquidity.[12]

Keynes postulated that the level of transactions undertaken by an individual and also by the aggregate of individuals would be in a stable relationship to the level of income. Hence, the so-called transactions demand for money would be proportional to the level of income. The use of the term "transactions motive," however, was confined to describing the necessity of holding cash to bridge the gap between the receipt of payments and the disbursement of such proceeds, or to bridge the interval between purchase and realization.

According to Keynes, the precautionary motive concerns the two aspects of the demand for balances: first, the demand for cash as a proportion of assets "to provide for contingencies requiring sudden expenditure and for unforeseen opportunities of advantageous purchases"; and second, the demand for an asset whose "value is fixed in terms of money to meet a subsequent liability (e.g., bank indebtedness) fixed in terms of money."[13] Keynes suggested that the demand for money arising from the precautionary motive would also depend largely on the level of income.

Marshall and Pigou suggested that uncertainty about the future was one of the factors that might be expected to influence the demand for money. Keynes' analysis of the speculative motive represents an attempt to formalize one aspect of this suggestion and to draw conclusions from it:

> The aggregate demand for money to satisfy the speculative motive usually shows a continuous response to gradual changes in the rate of interest[14]

Furthermore, he said, "it is important to distinguish between changes in the rate of interest . . . due to changes in the supply of money . . . and those which are primarily due to changes in expectations affecting the liquidity function itself."[15]

Accordingly, the Keynesian theory of liquidity preference separates the demand for money into two parts:

$$M^D = L_1(Y) + L_2(r) \qquad (17)$$

The first part, $L_1(Y)$, based on transactions and precautionary motives, is treated as a function of income; the second part, $L_2(r)$, is based on speculative motives as a function of the interest rate. This analytical breakthrough by Keynes was significant in that it placed the demand for money in a behavioral framework consistent with the concept of utility maximization in an uncertain world, and away from the restrictive notion of institutionally determined payment schedules. Later economists, however, have found that the demand for transactions balances was also interest elastic.[16] Since the alternative to holding cash for transaction purposes is short-run assets or time deposits, their rate of return should influence the money demand and the short-term rate of interest should be treated as an argument in the demand function for money.

Moreover, people's behavior in holding cash balances is affected not only by the transactions, precautionary, and speculative motives as dictated by the Keynesian theory, but also by their expectation of changes in the price level.[17] The alternative cost of carrying over one's wealth from one period to the next in the form of cash balances is the profit one could obtain by carrying over this wealth in the form of other assets, such as commodities and bonds.

> The profit that can be obtained by carrying over a bond is measured by the rate of interest. Similarly, the profit that can be obtained by carrying over commodities is measured by the anticipated rate of increase in prices. Hence just as we assume a negatively sloping demand curve for money as a function of the rate of interest, so can we assume one as the rate of price increase. In both cases the negative slope expresses the fact that the higher the alternative cost of holding cash balances, the smaller the amount demanded.[18]

The symmetry between the rate of interest and the rate of price increase brings out the fact that even the existence of certain anticipations of a price increase will not cause an absolute flight from cash. Instead, just as in the case of the interest rate, it will simply cause the individuals to adjust their holdings of real cash balances so that the marginal utility of the liquidity cash balances provide compensates individuals for the opportunity costs of holding these balances.[19]

Therefore, the expected rate of change of the price level must be interpreted as an expected rate of return on money holding. Other things being equal, the higher the expected rate of return to money holding, the more of it will be held; the lower it is, the less will be held. The expected rate of change of the price level becomes a potentially important variable in the demand-for-money function. Since the actual rate of change in prices of the immediate past is probably the basic determinant of present expected change in prices, for simplicity, the former may be substituted as an argument explaining the demand for money. The demand for money may assume the basic form:

$$M/P^D = f(r^s, Y/P, Z) \qquad (18)$$

Where M^D is nominal money stock, P is the price level, r^s is the short-term market rate of interest, Y/P is the real income, and $Z = (P - P_{-1})/P_{-1}$ is the rate of changes in the price level. In equation (1) partial derivatives of M^D/P with respect to r^s and Z are expected to be negative, and that with respect to Y/P to be positive.

SUPPLY OF MONEY

The pure theory of the demand for money assumes that the nominal supply of money is given and is varied at the discretion of the monetary authorities and government. Demand theory sets out to analyze the effects on general equilibrium of a change in the nominal quantity of money or of a change in demand for money arising from an exogenous change in tastes. Demand theory also explicitly assumes that the monetary authorities and government can control the nominal quantity of money. In contrast to this view, there is a school that sees the money supply responding to demand; it therefore concludes that there is no point in attempting to control the economy by monetary policy. Hence, a theory of money, if it is to be consistent, requires that supply be determined independently of the money demand, and if the theory is to be of use, it must allow that the central bank can control the quantity of money in the hands of the public.[20]

Early theories of money supply developed a mechanistic approach that did not allow for the possibility of ratios being behavioral functions of economic variables. This stage of the theory's development is evocative of early quantity theory and Keynesian multiplier analysis. There is now considerable evidence showing that the supply of money can be expressed as a function of a few variables.[21] Basically, these functions are two types. First, Brunner (1961) and Brunner and Meltzer (1963) consider money supply as a function of the monetary base, currency-deposit ratio, and reserve-deposit ratio. They contend that, with the monetary base given, the current rate of interest can have very little effect on the supply of money. Second, in contrast, Teigen (1964), Goldfeld (1966), Smith (1967), Modigliani, Rasche, and Cooper (1970), and Bhattacharya (1974) attach importance to the interest rates. A bank's ability to vary the level of excess and borrowed reserves it wishes to hold provides an important reason for treating the money supply as an endogenous variable. The interest responsiveness of excess and borrowed reserves implies a supply function of money that is similarly responsive. To allow this dependence, Teigen has estimated a relationship in which the money supply is made a function of certain Federal Reserve parameters and of interest rates. While the study by Goldfeld is a "slightly high-order approach" in that he derives the money supply from bank behavior, a function of the Teigen-type is implicit in his model. In particular:

When studies of money-supply determination are reviewed, two main theories emerge. One is that in general there is a stable relationship between the money supply and the reserve base, so that when the stock of reserves increases or decreases, the money supply will change in a predictable way. According to this theory, therefore, a central bank can control the money supply by controlling total reserves or the banking and monetary system. The other main theory is that in the United States, the volume of member banks borrowing from the Federal Reserve System and the volume of excess reserves of the member banks(or the net of these two in 'free' reserves) influence bank behavior in such a way that the rate of change of bank deposits and money supply can be predicted from these variables. An implication of the second main theory for the operation of a central bank is that attention should be focused on excess reserves and borrowings, or on free reserves, rather than on total reserves in attempting to control the money supply.[22]

The two main theories are not so clearly alternative to one another as they might seem to be at first. Each contains useful insights regarding the behavior of the monetary system. If they are combined, each may contribute an essential element of a more satisfactory explanation of changes in money supply than can be obtained from either of them separately.

In this section, we will develop a way to incorporate variation in excess reserves and borrowings, or the two combined in free reserves, in a theory of money supply determination. By so doing, we synthesize the two basic approaches described above.

The derivation of the money supply model proceeds as follows: monetary base (H), or high-powered money as it is frequently referred to, is defined to include all monetary assets capable of being used as banking reserves. It is represented by

$$H = C + R \tag{19}$$

where R = high-powered money inside the banks (banking reserves), and C = high-powered money outside the banks (currently supplied by the government). C is defined as

$$C = C_p + C_b \tag{20}$$

where C_p = currency held by the nonbank public, and C_b = currency held by commercial banks.

In the United States, currency held by commercial banks (vault cash) can also be counted as required reserves. It can also be used for excess reserves. In this case, high-powered money is defined as

$$H = C_p + R \tag{21}$$

where total bank reserves (R) are then defined as

$$R = R_r + R_e + C_b. \tag{22}$$

In either case, the definition of high-powered money is not changed.

Similarly, total bank reserves are defined as

$$R = R_r + R_e \tag{23}$$

where R_r = required reserves of member banks, and R_e = excess reserves of member banks. Money supply is defined as

$$M^s{}_1 = C_p + DD \tag{24}$$

or

$$M^s{}_2 = C_p + D \tag{24'}$$

where DD refers to demand deposits and D the sum of demand and time deposits.

Regardless of whether definition (24) or (24′) of money supply is used, the arguments will remain the same. But the data on R_r will be different for demand deposits and aggregate deposits. Without loss of generality, if we further assume that the public desires to hold a fixed proportion g(O<gl) of money supply in currency, and that the banking system maintains a fixed cash-deposit ratio n (O<n<1), then we get

$$C_p = g_1 M^s{}_1 \tag{25}$$

or

$$C_p = g_2 M^s{}_2 \tag{25'}$$

and

$$C_b = n_1 DD = n_1(M^s{}_1 - C_1 = n_1(1-g)M^s{}_1 \tag{26}$$

or

$$C_b = n_2 D = n_2(M^s{}_2 - C_p) = n_2(1-g)M_s{}^2. \tag{27}$$

If k is the required reserve ratio $(O<k<1)$, then we can write

$$R_r = k_1 DD = k_1(M_s{}^1 - C_p) \tag{28}$$

or

$$R_r = k_2 D = k_2(M^s{}_2 - C_p). \tag{28'}$$

Here we note that if k, g, and n are constant, the authorities can control the money supply by fixing monetary base (H). But if H is held constant and k or g or n changes, then the money supply does not remain constant. The reserve-deposit ratio rises as commercial banks keep larger reserves to ensure solvency in the face of increased uncertainty.

Thus, the money supply at any moment is the result of portfolio decisions by the central bank, the commercial banks, and the public. Whether the central banks, by controlling the monetary base, can actually achieve fairly precise control over the money supply, depends on whether the link between the monetary base and bank reserves, and between bank reserves and the money supply (the monetary base-bank reserves-money supply linkage is fairly tight and therefore predictable). If there is a tight linkage, the monetary authorities can formulate their policies and achieve any particular target for the money supply; on the other hand, if there is significant unpredictable slippage, and the central bank control over the money supply is not sufficiently precise to achieve a given target, it will necessarily have to formulate its policies in terms of other variables it can control. The variable used to confine the central bank's objective, or to implement its policy decisions, must therefore be one it can control within reasonable limits.[23]

Let U be the unborrowed monetary base, defined as

$$U = H - R_b \tag{29}$$

where R_b refers to the borrowings by commercial banks from the central bank. Then, from (2^2) through (9^2), we obtain

$$U_1 = C_p + C_b + R_b + (R_e - R_b) = (g + n - ng + k - kg)M^s{}_1 + R_f \tag{30}$$

$$U_2 = (g + n - ng + k - kg)M_s{}^2 + R_f \tag{30'}$$

where $R_f = R_e - R_b$ is free reserves.

"Free reserves" are used in this discussion rather than the component "excess reserves" and "borrowings" in part for convenience in exposition and in part because there are plausible theoretical grounds for this procedure. The question of whether excess reserves and borrowings should be treated separately or as combined in free reserves will be kept open.

Member banks hold excess reserves because they want to be able to meet the cash demands of their depositors without drawing down their legal reserves and hence incurring a penalty cost on reserve deficiencies. Excess reserves, however, are assumed non-earning assets. The opportunity cost to the banks is the yield they must give up by not acquiring an earning asset such as government securities.

Banks are supposedly discouraged from borrowing from the central bank except to meet unexpected short-term contingencies. Nevertheless, there is some interest elasticity with respect to the discount rate.[24] If the discount rate is substantially below the yield that can be earned on short-term government securities, commercial banks will prefer to borrow from the central bank instead of selling these securities. Thus, the lower the discount rate relative to short-term market interest rates, the lower will be the level of free reserves if the central bank does not take off-setting measures. That is, the level of the discount rate determines to some extent whether banks sell short-term securities or draw down their excess reserves.

> Banks will prefer to decrease their reserves by a greater amount the larger the (positive) spread between short-term interest rates and the discount rate, and they will sell more bills the smaller this spread. Because there is often considerable hesitancy about continued borrowing from the Fed, one would not expect the effects of changes in each interest rate to be symmetrical. A change of 1 percent in the short-term rate should have a greater effect on banks' reserve position than a change of 1 percent in the discount rate. . . . But changes in both rates exert an influence on bank behavior.[25]

Without specifying the direction of causality between the discount rate and the short-term interest rate, the free reserves function can be treated as a function of the discount rate (r^d) and the short-term market rate of interest (r^s).[26] Free reserves will also vary with the lagged reserve ratio of commercial banks, v_{-1}, defined as the ratio of the holdings of reserves by banks to their deposit at the beginning of each year. v_{-1} is a lagged endogenous variable, as its components are all determined within the system.[27] These considerations suggest that the free reserves function may assume the basic form

$$R_f = h^* \, (r^d, r^s, v_{-1}). \tag{31}$$

In equation (31) partial derivatives of R_f with respect to r^d and v_{-1} are expected to be positive, and those with respect to r^s to be negative. Combining equations (21) and (22) and solving for $M^s{}_q$, $q = 1,2$, we obtain the basic form of money supply function

$$M^s{}_q = h(U, r^d, r^s, v_{-1}). \tag{32}$$

In equation (32) partial derivatives of $M^s{}_q$ with respect to U and r^s are expected to be positive, and those with respect to r^d and v_{-1} to be negative.

If free reserves are assumed to be linear of the basic form

$$R_f = a_0 + a_2 r^d - a_3 r^s + a_4 v_{-1} \tag{33}$$

then we get the money supply function as

$$M^s{}_q = l/m(-a_o + a_1 U = a_2 r^d + a_3 r^s - a_4 v_{-1}) \tag{34}$$

where $q = 1,2$, and $m = (g + n - ng + k - kg)$.

The money supply function postulated in equation (34) differs from the money supply functions derived by Teigen and others. Teigen has distinguished the actual from the potential money supply. But this is not the case of equation (34). It also differs from that of Bhattacharya, who has introduced the differential between the discount rate and a short-term market interest rate as an explicit variable.

THE MONETARY APPROACH TO THE BALANCE-OF-PAYMENTS

The reemergence of the long dormant view, with roots going back more than two hundred years, that money and monetary policy are indeed important is underscored by the work on the monetary approach to the balance-of-payments undertaken by James Meade, Harry Johnson, Robert Mundell, Jacob Frankel, J. Richard Zecher, Bluford H. Putman, D. Sykes Wilford, and others. This approach can be summarized in the proposition that the balance-of-payments is essentially a monetary phenomenon:

In general the approach emphasizes the budget constraint imposed on a country's international spending and views the various accounts of the balance-of-payments as the "windows" to the outside world, through which excesses of domestic flow demands over domestic flow supplies are cleared. Accordingly, surpluses in the grade account and the capital account, respectively, represent excess flow supplies of goods and of securities, and a surplus in the money account reflects an excess domestic flow demand for money. Consequently, in analyzing the money account, or more familiarly the rate of increase or decrease in the country's international reserves, the monetary approach focuses on the determinants of the excess domestic flow demand for a supply of money.[28]

Though the approach is described as "monetary," it should not be confused with the term "monetarist" used in policy debates, especially over the use of monetary policy as contrasted with fiscal policy in economic stabilization. As Johnson and Frankel put it:

The monetary approach to the balance-of-payments asserts neither that monetary mismanagement is the only cause, nor that monetary policy change is the only possible cure, to balance-of-payments problems; it does suggest, however, that monetary processes will bring about a cure of some kind—not necessarily very attractive—unless frustrated by deliberate monetary policy action, and that policies that neglect or aggravate the monetary implications of deficits and surpluses will not be successful in their declared objectives.[29]

As in the quantity theory statement of Milton Friedman, the essential assumption in the monetary approach is that there does exist an aggregate demand function for money that is a stable function of a relatively small number of aggregate economic variables. In this sense, it makes the same assumptions as in the moderate Keynesian view. Like the classical quantity theory of money, the monetary approach assumes the longer run view, for the most part, of a fully employed economy as the norm rather than the exception.

A country's size is irrelevant to the monetary approach. A small country viewed as facing a parametric set of world prices and interest rates presents no theoretical difficulty in taking demand and supply functions as dependent on prices rather than prices themselves as parameters. Johnson and Frankel note that country size is important on the monetary side of analysis. For instance, a large country such as the United States whose national currency is internationally acceptable may, as a result of following an inflationary domestic credit policy, force an accumulation of its money in foreign hands and so lead to world inflation rather than a loss in its international reserves. The postwar era is a good illustration of such a case.

Of the several studies reported on by Harry Johnson up to about 1975, one is by N. Parkin, I. Richards, and G. Zis (1975):

> [An] empirical study of the determination and control of the world money supply under fixed exchange rates (1961–1971) reaches the important general conclusions that the growth of the world money supply in the study period was influenced in an important and predictable way by the growth of the world reserve money, but that even if there had been firm control of the growth of world high-powered money, this would not have prevented national control banks from pursuing domestic credit expansion policies unconducive to world price stability.[30]

Zecher properly put the issues in perspective when he writes that

> The emergence of the monetary approach in the late 1960s and 1970s marks a major swing in economic thought back to the concepts of Hume and Smith, and away from the balance-of-payments theories that emerged from the Keynesian revolution. . . . At the same time, domestic monetarism was a rising force, emphasizing the importance of money and the general equilibrium nature of domestic economies. Given that world goods and capital markets were becoming more and more integrated, international theorists were forced to rework their models; simultaneously, the importance of monetary demand and supply relationships on a world level was becoming integrated with this new general equilibrium approach to balance-of-payments questions.[31]

NOTES

1. John R. Hicks, "The Keynes Centenary: A Skeptical Follower," *The Economist* (June 18, 1983): pp. 17–9.

2. Ibid., p. 17.

3. Ibid., p. 18.

4. Ibid., p. 18.

5. Ibid., p. 18.

6. Milton Friedman, "A Theoretical Framework for Monetary Analysis," *Journal of Political Economy* (April/May 1970): pp. 193–238; Milton Friedman, "A Monetary Theory of National Income," *Journal of Political Economy* (April/May 1971): pp. 323–37; see also George Macesich, *Monetarism: Theory and Policy* (New York: Praeger, 1983): pp. 43–60.

7. See George Macesich, *Monetarism: Theory and Policy*, Chapter 7.

8. Friedman, "A Theoretical Framework for Monetary Analysis," *Journal of Political Economy* (April/May 1970): pp. 193–238.

9. Friedman, "A Monetary Theory of National Income," Journal of Political Economy (1970): pp. 323–37.

10. Ibid., pp. 323–37.

11. H. P. Minsky argues in "Central Banking and Money Market Changes," *Quarterly Journal of Economics*, 67 (May 1957) that innovation in the money market may be responsible for such shifts. On the other hand, Scott E. Hein, "Dynamic Forecasting and the Demand for Money," *Federal Reserve Bank of St. Louis Review* (June/July 1980): pp. 13–23, rejects the notion of a constantly shifting money demand relationship and concludes that money is a useful policy instrument. Innovation has had little effect on the demand for money over the past decade.

12. John Maynard Keynes, *The General Theory of Employment, Interest and Money* (New York: Harcourt, Brace, 1936): p. 194.

13. Ibid., pp. 170–71, 195–97.

14. Ibid., p. 197.

15. Ibid., p. 197.

16. In his later writings, Keynes did permit the rates of interest to affect $L_1()$ as well as $L_2()$; see his "Theory of the Rate of Interest" (1937), reprinted in *Readings in the Theory of Income Distribution*, W. Feller and B. F. Healey, eds. (Philadelphia: The Blakiston Co., 1949): p. 422.

17. Milton Friedman, "The Demand for Money—Some Theoretical and Empirical Results," *Journal of Political Economy* 67 (June 1959): pp. 327–51; R. Selden, "Monetary Velocity in the United States," in Milton Friedman, ed., *Studies in the Quantity Theory of Money* (Chicago: University of Chicago Press, 1956); D. Laidler, *The Demand for Money: Theories and Evidence* (Scranton, Pa.: International Textbook, 1969):

pp. 106–97; Lawrence B. Smith and John W. L. Winder, "Price and Interest Rate Expectations and the Demand for Money in Canada," *Journal of Finance* (June 1979): pp. 671–82.

18. Don Patinkin, *Money, Interest, and Prices*, 2d ed. (New York: Harper & Row, 1965): pp. 144–45.

19. Ibid., p. 145. The interested reader may profitably look into Patinkin's other studies dealing with one or another aspect of Keynesian economics. See Patinkin, *Keynes' Monetary Thought* (Durham: Duke University Press, 1976); Patinkin and J. Clark Leita, eds. *Keynes, Cambridge and the General Theory* (Toronto: University of Toronto Press, 1978).

20. Harry G. Johnson, *Macroeconomics and Monetary Theory* (London: Gray-Mills, 1971): p. 135.

21. For a survey of this evidence, refer to A. J. Meigs, *Free Reserves and the Money Supply* (Chicago: University of Chicago Press, 1962); P. H. Hendershoot and F. DeLeeuw, "Free Reserves, Interest Rates and Deposits: A Synthesis," *Journal of Finance* 25 (June 1970): pp. 599–614; Macesich and Tsai, *Money in Economic Systems*.

22. Meigs, *Free Reserves*: p. 1.

23. David I. Fand, "Some Issues in Monetary Economics," *Federal Reserve Bank of St. Louis Review* (January 1970). It is for this reason that we have treated the unborrowed monetary base as the policy variable.

24. Goldfeld, *Commercial Banking Behavior and Economic Activity: A Structural Study of Monetary Policy in the Post-war United States* (Amsterdam: North-Holland Publishing Co., 1966): pp. 43–50.

25. Michael K. Evans, *Macroeconomic Activity* (New York: Harper & Row, 1969): pp. 314–15.

26. The relationship between free reserves and the interest rates and the discount rates developed here is analogous to that by Meigs (1962), Goldfeld (1966), Teigen (1964), and Bhattacharya (1974). Based on his empirical evidence, Meigs concludes that the free reserves ratio is functionally related to market rate of interest and the discount rate. Bhattacharya assumes free reserves to be an increasing function of the differential between the discount rate and a short-term market rate of interest. If anything, borrowing is sometimes held to be a function of that differential. If that differential widens, banks may borrow additional funds, but they do not necessarily retain those funds as resources.

27. The studies that have related quantities of reserves supplied to the banking system to changes in volume of earning assets or deposits of the banks are: Balance Sheet of Banking, 1953–55," *Journal of Finance* 12 (May 1957): pp. 238–55; Allan H. Meltzer, "The Behavior of the French Money Supply: 1938–54," *Journal of Political Economy* 67 (June 1959):

pp. 275–96; Stephen L. McDonald, "The Internal Drain and Bank Credit Expansion," *Journal of Finance*, 7 (December 1953): pp. 407–21. An extensive discussion bearing on the reserve ratio and free reserves is given by Albert E. Burger, *The Money Supply Process* (Belmont, Calif.: Wadsworth, 1971): pp. 24–72. Reference should also be made to A. James Meigs' (1962) discussion on free reserves and the money supply.

28. See papers in Jacob A. Frankel and Harry G. Johnson, eds. *The Monetary Approach to the Balance of Payments* (London: George Allen and Unwin, 1978); Bluford H. Putman and D. Sykes Wilford, eds. *The Monetary Approach to International Adjustment* (New York: Praeger, 1978) contains useful theoretical and empirical studies on the monetary approach to international adjustment, as well as a statement by J. Richard Zecher and a bibliography of relevant studies. See also George Macesich, *The International Monetary Economy and the Third World* (New York: Praeger, 1981), Chapters 2 and 3; Macesich and Tsai, *Money in Economic Systems*, Chapter 11.

29. Frankel and Johnson, "The Monetary Approach to the Balance of Payments: Essential Concepts and Historical Origins," in *The Monetary Approach to the Balance of Payments*: p. 21.

30. Harry G. Johnson, "Monetary Approach to the Balance-of-Payments: A Nontechnical Guide," in John Adams, ed. *The Contemporary International Economy: A Reader* (New York: St. Martin's Press, 1979): p. 205. The empirical study is N. Parkin, I. Richards, and G. Zis, "The Determination and Control of the World Money Supply under Fixed Exchange Rates, 1961–71," *Manchester School* 43 (September 1975): pp. 293–316.

31. J. Richard Zecher, *Preface to Monetary Approach to International Adjustment*: pp. ix–x.

Chapter 9

Democratic Market Society

A MANAGED MONETARY STANDARD

In his search for a workable monetary standard, Keynes founded in the *General Theory*, according to Hicks, the labor standard and its dependence on society's sociopolitical processes. Because of other things, this translated into a "managed monetary standard" and justification for its discretionary management by central monetary authorities composed of an "enlightened elite."

Keynes' efforts were translated into a "managed monetary standard" and yielded readily to discretionary monetary manipulation by authorities. The consequent monetary uncertainty generated by such manipulation has had the effect on balance of casting doubt on the credibility of these authorities, their policies, and ultimately on the monetary regime itself. In the process, the long-term price level has lost its anchor. These are only the more obvious unintended consequences of Keynes' efforts.

The unintended consequences of Keynes' search for a workable monetary standard are but another illustration of money in history and the unintended effects of human actions and decisions which have had perverse effects. The best intentional changes do at times lead via unintended consequences to undesirable results. Keynes' efforts are no exception.

Indeed, the idea that the unintended effects of human actions and decisions often have unforeseen consequences came into currency in the eighteenth century at about the same time that another idea confidently supported the belief that institutional changes can be so engineered as to bring about a perfect society.[1] The idea of the perfectability of the social order arose primarily in the course of the French Enlightenment while that of the unintended consequences was a principal contribution of the contemporary Scottish moralists.

The idea of a perfectable society is deeply imbedded in critiques of social and economic order. By the beginning of the nineteenth century, the idea served to launch strong criticism of capitalism and the social and economic order it represented. In the twentieth century, the idea also served Keynes in his search for a workable monetary standard.

In fact, Keynes' flexibility and fine tuning propensities are certainly consistent with ideas flowing from the French Enlightenment. His propensities, writes Friedman, "were in accord with his elitist political philosophy, his conception of society run by an able corps of public spirited intellectuals entitled to power that they could be counted on to exercise for the masses. They may also have been related to an excessive confidence on his ability to shape public opinion."[2] His flexibility and attribution to others of his own capacity to change his views by changing circumstances also led to serious misreading of matters far removed from economic policy.[3]

An example of Keynes' flexibility and misreading of events is provided by Hayek when he writes, "I am convinced that he owed his extraordinary influence in this field [economics], to which he [Keynes] gave only a small part of his energy, to an almost unique combination of other gifts." He had gained the ear of the "advanced" numbers much earlier and greatly contributed to a trend very much in conflict with his own classical liberal beginnings. The time when he had become the idol of the leftist intellectuals was in fact when in 1933 he had shocked many of his earlier admirers by an essay on "National Self-Sufficiency" in the *New Statesman and Nation* (reprinted with equal enthusiasm by the *Yale Review*, the *Communist Science and Society* and the *National Socialist* Schmollers Jahrbuch).[4]

In the essay in question, Hayek quotes Keynes: "The decadent international but individualistic capitalism, in the hands of which we found ourselves after the war is not a success. It is not intelligent, it is not beautiful, it is not just, it is not virtuous—and it does not deliver the goods. In short, we dislike it and are beginning to despise it." And, writes Hayek, Keynes later, in the same mood, states in the preface to the German translation of the *General*

Theory that "he [Keynes] frankly recommended his policy proposals as being more easily adapted to the conditions of a totalitarian state than those in which production is guided by free competition."[5]

SELF-DESTRUCTION THESIS

Criticism of capitalism's shortcomings is a view that Keynes shared with other contemporaries. Keynes, of course, was also a man with a very sharp sense of history, theory, and policy. In chapter 24 "Concluding Notes on the Social Philosophy Towards Which the General Theory Might Lead" of his *General Theory*, he writes that "the authoritarian state systems of today seem to solve the problem of unemployment at the expense of efficiency and of freedom. But it may be possible by a right analysis of the problem to cure the disease whilst preserving efficiency and freedom."[6]

Keynes, the liberal economist, was certainly well aware of the advantages and value of individualism and the capitalist market system. Thus, he writes, "Whilst, therefore, the enlargement of the functions of government, involved in the task of adjusting to one another the propensity to consume and the inducement to invest would seem . . . both the only practicable means of avoiding the destruction of existing economic forms in their entirety and the condition of the successful functioning of individual initiative."[7]

In effect, Keynes felt that shortcomings of the capitalist market-oriented individualist system could be overcome with appropriate policies of government intervention while at the same time preserving the system's efficiency and freedom. On this point, Keynes is consistent with the eighteenth century view that social engineering via appropriate government policies can improve society's lot. And, indeed, Keynes is also consistent with the "self-destruction thesis" of capitalism discussed by Albert Hirschman and many other writers past and present including conservatives and Marxists.[8]

As we discussed earlier, Fred Hirsch in developing a version of the "self-destruction thesis" argues that capitalism depletes or erodes the moral foundation needed for its functioning.[9] Keynesian bureaucratic elite, as we have argued, assume an increasingly important roll in managing the system.

They must be motivated by the "general interest" rather than "self-interest." The system, however, is based on self-interest and provides no clear way of generating the proper "general interest." To the extent that such a motivation does exist, it is a residue of previous value systems that are likely to erode.

As we noted, Keynes, Lippman, and others avoid the problems of implementation arising as a consequence of potential conflict between "general interest" and self-interest" by arguing in favor of an enlightened elite of bureaucratic managers who would carry out the required program. The net result is that collective objectives are superimposed on an individualistic calculus. Though Great Britain may have favored the paternalism of Keynes' elite democracy, America does not.

And, indeed, as we have had occasion to note, more drastic treatment may be required if capitalism is to be saved. According to Hirsch, for instance, the capitalist market undermines the moral values that are its own supports. These supports have been inherited from preceding socioeconomic regimes, such as feudalism. The social morality which serves to buttress the market draws on an earlier morality which has eroded over time and by the very operation of the market itself. The greater mobility and anonymity of an industrial market-oriented capitalist society has increasingly directed individual behavior to individual advantage, habits, and instincts at the expense of communal attitudes and objectives. The consequent weakening of traditional values has made the capitalist market-oriented economy increasingly more difficult to manage.

Such social virtues as truth, trust, acceptance, restraint, obligation, argues Hirsch, are needed for the functioning of an individualistic, contractual economy.[10] To a good measure, continues Hirsch, these virtues are based on religious belief which the individualistic, rationalistic orientation of a capitalist market economy undermines.[11]

Religious belief, however, is not what earlier writers of the seventeenth and eighteenth centuries had taken as characteristic of man. They were more realistic in viewing "self-interest" rather than "love and charity" as the basis for a well-ordered society.[12] Moreover, they expected that the market would generate rather than erode such desired moral values as trust, truth, and other prerequisites required in a contractual society. It was expected that contract would replace custom, the traditional and ancient by the modern as a result of the pervasive influence and driving force of the market.

It could be, as Hirschman tells us, that to credit the market and capitalism with extraordinary powers of expansion, penetration, and disintegration "may in fact have been an adroit ideological maneuver for intimating that it was headed for disaster."[13]

Hirschman goes on to argue that the simplest model for the self-destruction of capitalism is one that presents the idea that the successful attainment of wealth will undermine the process of wealth generation. Accordingly, the advance of capitalism requires "first capitalists save and lead a frugal life so that accumulation can proceed apace. However, at some ill-defined point, increases in wealth resulting from successful accumulation will tend to enervate the spirit of frugality. Demands will be made for *la dolce vita*, that is for instance, rather than delayed gratification and when that happens capitalist progress will grind to a halt."[14]

Indeed, the idea that the rise and decline of capitalism occurs as a consequence of at first a successful attainment of wealth and of subsequently a deterioration in the wealth-creating process is a familiar eighteenth century theme found in such writers as John Wesley Montesquieu and Adam Smith.[15] More modern versions of the theme are found in Max Weber's essay on *The Protestant Ethic*, as well as in Herbert Marcuse and Daniel Bell.

The basic flaw in the idea, according to Hirschman, is that it focuses on the generation and the decline in personal savings while overlooking the more strategic variables, such as corporate savings, technical innovation, entrepreneurial skills, as well as cultural and institutional factors.

A more sophisticated version of the self-destruction hypothesis is put forward by Joseph Schumpeter.[16] Accordingly, capitalism generates a critical frame of mind which after destroying the moral authority of many institutions turns upon itself and destroys the supporting values so necessary to a viable bourgeois society. And it is the intellectuals who spearhead the attack on capitalism. This overlooks, however, the system's strength at mounting a vigorous defense and counterattack. On this score, capitalism has managed its forces very well indeed (e.g., counter-cyclical policies, employment, and social security legislation), in turning aside system-threatening attacks on the part of intellectuals and others.

Hirschman argues that Schumpeter's thesis may be made more appealing if it can be demonstrated that the ideological currents unleashed by capitalism inadvertently erode the moral foundations of capitalism.[17] That is, if it can be shown that somehow capitalism is much more dependent on the previous system's "social and ideological foundations than realized by the conquering bourgeoisie and their ideologies, their demolition work will have the *incidental* result of weakening the foundations on which they themselves are sitting. This idea was developed by a very different group of European intellectuals who had also come to the United States during the 1930s: the Frankfurt School of Critical Theory which, while working in the Marxist tradition, paid considerable attention to ideology as a crucial factor in historical development."[18]

Essentially, the idea is that a self-interest oriented capialist society depletes its moral legacy. Reason in such a society serves merely as a means for achieving arbitrary ends while leaving little to say about shaping human ends. The previous interaction between reason and revelation has been eroded by the progress of a utilitarian philosophy and a self-interest oriented capitalist society. In effect, the formalization of reason has served to undermine such cherished ideas as humanity and freedom which have served to hold society together. These values, moreover, have been inherited from previous social and ideological regimes.

It is interesting that Hirschman argues that capitalist society has been saved from its self-destructive proclivities by Keynesianism, planning, and welfare state reforms. It is not surprising, according to Hirschman, that the self-destruction thesis arose at the more difficult years of the twentieth century. Certainly the 1920s, 1940s, and the late 1960s and 1970s were years of troubles. What is surprising is the failure to link these "somber ideas about self-destruction arose at the more difficult and somber moments of our century, but that there was a failure to connect them with earlier more hopeful expectations of a market society bringing forth its own moral foundation, via the generation of *douceur*, probity, trust. One reason for this lack of contact is the low profile of the *doux-commerce* thesis after its period of self-confidence in the preceding century. Another is the transfiguration of that thesis into one in which it was hard to recognize."[19]

The Industrial Revolution and its upheaval had much to do with casting into doubt the *doux* (soft, gentle) nature of the thesis. Except in international trade where expanding trade and contacts were expected to produce mutual material and cultural gains, domestic expansion of trade and industry was widely viewed as bringing about chaos, disintegration of communities, and a general breakdown in social and moral values. Thus, the force which was released in the center of capitalism came to be viewed as wild, blind, relentless, and unbridled.[20]

Others continued to push forth the view that, on the contrary, society was indeed held together by the network of mutual obligations and relations arising out of the market.[21] It is not simply as a result of self-interested market transactions but the division of labor that holds society together. And it is primarily the unintended consequences of people's actions and commitments in the wake of market transactions that play the critical role. In effect, a comprehensive system of rights and duties is created by the division of labor which serves to tie members of society together.

There is in this view, as Hirschman underscores, a certain ambivalence on law, in fact a "solidarity" society emerges from the division of labor. The view appears to be "caught between the older view that interest-oriented action provides a basis for social integration and the more contemporary critique of market society as . . . corrosive of social cohesion."[22] There is to be sure an advantage to such ambivalence and the idea that under favorable conditions social bonds can be attached to economic transactions.

It is to the work of Georg Simmel and our earlier discussion that we must turn for the important role that money, credit, competition, and the market play in society. Competition and the market play significant roles in providing empathy and promoting strong social bonds in society. To Simmel, competition in society is always in favor of a third party. Each of the competitors tries to come as close as possible to the interests of the third party. Modern competition is for Simmel a fight of all against all and at the same time, a fight for all. It provides a vast network for the formation of third party interests. And indeed, if we take it that the third party to competition among producers is the consumer and that everyone is a consumer, society as a whole is well served by it.

As we have discussed earlier, Simmel's views on recovery and credit stressed their importance in the functioning of the economy. In good measure, it results in their promotion of trust in social relations. This feature of the market along with competition serves to make social integration a reality. It provides in good part the bonds that for earlier societies were supplied by custom and religion.

INFLATION AND DEMOCRACY

The managed monetary standard in the form of a labor standard and its dependence in democracies on society's sociopolitical processes has promoted bureaucracy and centralization beyond anything Keynes and his followers probably intended. Another consequence appears to be the upward trend of prices since World War II which is facilitated by a growing preoccupation and sensitivity to *any* unemployment.[23] This sensitivity is now in fact institutionalized in the Employment Act of 1946.

The apparent declining effectiveness of policy restraints in democracies to postwar increases in the general level of prices has cast doubt on monetary authorities and the monetary regime itself, permitting inflation to feed on its own strength. To be sure, if the inflation rate is constant and widely expected and if the economy adjusts completely, the principal disadvantage appears to be the inability to compensate holders of currency for the losses in purchasing power—power due to inflation which can be viewed as expropriation of resources such holders would otherwise command. The matter is now more complicated when inflation is anticipated. Since actual rates of inflation are too volatile to be anticipated with any degree of accuracy, the uncertainty of inflation rates imposes major costs in reduced efficiency of production and resource allocation and in suboptimal saving and investment decisions.

The political attractiveness of inflation cannot be denied. In democracies, the task of incurring unemployment for the sake of reducing inflation can resolve political pressures to expand expenditures without legislating higher tax rates. Large continuing budget deficits could be financed without inflationary policies, but in practice, they are partially monetized, thus producing inflation in part because of pressures to hold down interest rates. It provides additional incentives to politically weak governments for providing an automatic reallocation of government expenditures in real terms without explicit legislative action, since rising prices reduce the real value of monetary allocations for which no increase is mandated. Thus, the government by pressure groups and through inaction allows all others to decline in real terms without the necessity of explicitly legislating monetary cutbacks in any expenditures.

Attempts to use manipulative monetary policy to achieve unattainable goals push the economy into the area of increasing inflationary pressures. It is an unattractive economic policy because the costs, for instance, of delaying a reduction of inflation are not compensated by lower overall costs of unemployment. It serves, moreover, to undermine the foundations on which the American democratic society rests.

Much of our discussion is implicit in the work by Alexis de Tocqueville on democracy more than a century and a half ago.[24] He predicted that democracy might usher in the control of a vast bureaucracy taking its sustenance from a majoritarian tyranny.

Unlike the critics of his time, de Tocqueville did not completely share their belief that democracy would bring mediocrity. In his view, the danger of democracy is the opportunity it gives to political and bureaucratic elites to multiply their power. Unlike the hierarchical societies of the past in which men had been tied to each other by the duty of obedience to superiors and of protection for inferiors which produced aristocrats with the inclination to challenge overmighty government and the power to do so, democratic man by contrast cannot. The reason he cannot, argued de Tocqueville, is because democratic man is surrounded by equals to whom he felt no ties of duty; on the contrary, democratic society made every man a rival.

According to de Tocqueville, two consequences flowed from this competitive individualism. The first was that the competition might absorb all energies, leaving none aside for political concerns. Second, democratic man would not be able to count on his neighbors for support; he would be forced to turn to the state. The first consequence diminished the citizen's interest in restraining control power; the second gave him a positive motive to increase it. By encouraging stronger government, equality could easily prove inimical to individual liberty. He was, in effect, predicting the rise of the protective welfare state as well as the reaction to it that is currently eroding its scope.

A check to central government and authority is to be found and, as de Toqueville indicated, in local institutions which at least in the United States are natural bastions of democracy. This is not necessarily true elsewhere, particularly where local governments and institutions were traditionally dominated by aristocrats. It is perhaps for this reason that European democrats, for instance, favored the centralization of power and so hastened the development of powerful central governments.

The majoritarian tyranny that worried Madison and that Jefferson feared would extinguish individual liberty has seeds in the managed labor standard of Keynes. The dependence of such a standard on society's sociopolitical processes would certainly have troubled eighteenth century Enlightenment thinkers like Adams, Madison, and Montesquieu. Without constraints imposed on the discretionary manipulation of such a standard, the bureaucracy acting presumably in the name of the majority is free to act on its own. The worst fear of the framers of the Constitution is fulfilled—the spectacle of the greater number oppressing the lesser.

It is this very spectacle expressed now in economics and the expropriation of wealth through the manipulation of the monetary standard, in which the majority and minority are regarded as having mutually excluding interests, as indeed they were by the framers of the American Constitution, that European patterns of class conflict can erupt in democratic America.

The manipulation of the monetary standard undermines the idea and sense of property common to most Americans who see a connection between exertion and reward and thus support property as sacrosanct. It is this permeation of Lockean values which has sustained Americans to assume that they had a "natural" right to acquire and dispose of property. It has meant that the majority need not be feared and that American society could be held together without the imposition of strong central government and its allied bureaucratic apparatus.

Indeed, de Tocqueville argued that where property is protected and "equality of condition" prevails, arbitrary or despotic rule is less likely. This does not mean that tyranny is no longer an issue. It simply means, as de Tocqueville argued, that tyranny must be redefined as a social phenomenon which results from the rise of mass democracy. It is the threat of society which absorbs the individual so that he experiences no conscious self apart from social existence. Authority moves from the individual to society as a whole with the result that the whole idea of individual natural rights, a heritage of the Enlightenment, evaporates. In its place arises the authority of society as opposed to that of the state.

As the authority of society displaces the idea of individual rights—a process well understood by such Transcendentalists as Thoreau—power becomes more centralized as the individual fearing his isolation and self-doubts, identifies more and more with society and internalizes its rules. Imperceptively, the idea of a single authority directing all citizens slips naturally into their consciousness, as de Tocqueville puts it, without their giving the matter a thought. The net result is that man's original political freedom, the contract of sovereignty in which he submits to the institutions of the state, has been overwhelmed by the dynamics of society. What Locke and Montesquieu have provided in natural and historical rights with which man can resist the power of the state has in essence been taken over by social authority. De Tocqueville, in effect, brought forth a new source of tyranny in the form of social authority. The importance of maintaining the credibility of work in America cannot be minimized as de Tocqueville underscored. Most Americans take pride in their work and view it as a duty to their community. It serves as a means for gaining respect. Both classical and socialist thinkers have failed to see that in a liberal environment, a market society and democracy are compatible. To be sure, de Tocqueville stops short of romanticizing the entrepreneur and treating him as an Emersonian genius who defies all convention. He views Americans as possessing a practical intelligence that serves them well in understanding public affairs and the country's interests.

In America, he noted, one may not find great acts of self-sacrifice and duty as in Europe but small deeds that nonetheless do reflect public spiritedness. In the Old World, argued de Tocqueville, one hears of the beauty and dignity of virtue and the grandeur of sacrifice and duty; in the New, of the value of character, of natural interest of every individual in the good of society, and of "honesty as the best policy" in all transactions.

This new sense of virtue is not as noble as the classical theorists would have it, nonetheless, it is more understandable and thus perhaps more realizable as de Tocqueville observed. It is moreover enlightened self-interest that yields "virtuous materialism" that most Americans can grasp. It is furthermore "wonderfully agreeable to human weakness" and thus can command authority. Enlightened self-interest, he observed, cannot make a man virtuous "but its discipline shapes a lot of orderly, temperate, moderate, careful, and self-controlled citizens. If it does not lead the will directly to virtue, it establishes habits which unconsciously turn it that way."[25]

As we have discussed, a monetary standard that does not lend itself to manipulation is a basic requirement if a democratic market society is to be well served. We leave it for our public-choice theory and accumulated experience that little trust can be given government, subject as it is to majority rule, to behave itself and exercise monetary restraint. In fact, the world has turned from the discipline of the gold standard to one of discretionary fiat money with now managed flexible exchange rates. Given the poor record that the current monetary regime has produced in high and variable inflation and interest rates, low productivity growth and unstable exchange rates has prompted a call for monetary reform involving a return to the gold standard.

There is, unfortunately, little ground for belief that contemporary popular democracies and their political authorities are willing to forego discretionary policies that a return to the gold standard or, for that matter, the establishment of a fiat money regime governed by a rule would require.

Unless the underlying political economy can guarantee that inflation will now be a policy option, neither a well-designed gold standard nor a rule-based fiat monetary regime requirement will be successful. The basic issue as discussed in this book is the degree of discretion that should be granted to the monetary authorities. A democratic market society, to function and survive, must have a predictable monetary policy capable of anchoring the long-term price level.

NOTES

1. See Albert Hirschman, "Rival Interpretations of Market Society: Civilizing, Destructive, or Feeble?" *Journal of Economic Literature* (December 1982): pp. 1463–84.

2. Milton Friedman, "The Keynes Centenary: A Monetarist Reflects," *The Economist* (June 4, 1983): p. 17.

3. Ibid., p. 18.

4. F. A. Hayek, "The Keynes Centenary: The Austrian Critique," *The Economist* (June 11, 1983): p. 41.

5. Ibid.

6. J. M. Keynes, *The General Theory of Employment, Interest, and Money* (New York: Harcourt, Brace, and World, Inc., First Harbinger Edition, 1964): p. 381.

7. Ibid., p. 380.

8. See his discussion in Hirschman, "Rival Interpretations of Market Society,": p. 1466.

9. Fred Hirsch, *Social Limits to Growth* (Cambridge: Harvard University Press, 1976) Second printing 1977: pp. 123–36.

10. Ibid., p. 141.

11. Ibid., p. 143.

12. Hirschman, "Rival Interpretations of Market Society": p. 1467.

13. Ibid., p. 1468.

14. Ibid.

15. Ibid.

16. Joseph Schumpeter, *Capitalism, Socialism, and Democracy* (New York: Harper, 1942).

17. Hirschman, "Rival Interpretations of Market Society": p. 1469.

18. Ibid.

19. Ibid., p. 1470.

20. Ibid.

21. See the views of Emile Durkeim discussed by Hirschman, ibid., p. 1471.

22. Ibid.

23. See Phillip Cagan, *Persistent Inflation: Historical and Policy Essays* (New York: Columbia University Press, 1979).

24. Alexis de Tocqueville, *Democracy in America* (Garden City, New York: Doubleday, 1969).

25. Ibid., pp. 525–28.

Bibliography

Ahmad, K. U. "An Empirical Study of Politico-Economic Interaction in the U.S.: A Comment." *Review of Economics and Statistics* (February 1983): 173–78.

Allen, Stuart D. "The Federal Reserve and the Electoral Cycle." *Journal of Money, Credit and Banking* (February 1986): 88–94.

Anderson, L. "The State of the Monetarist Debate." *Federal Reserve Bank of St. Louis Review* (December 1978).

Appleby, Joyce. *Capitalism and a New Social Order: The Republic Vision of the 1790's.* New York: New York University Press, 1984.

Auerbach, Robert D. *Money, Banking and Financial Markets*. New York: Macmillan Company, 1982: 362ff.

Bartley, Robert L. "Reagan in Command at a Crucible." *The Wall Street Journal* (January 28, 1986): 21.

Beck, N. "Presidential Influence on the Federal Reserve in the 1970's." *American Journal of Political Science* (August 1982): 415–45.

Bhattacharya, B. B. "Demand and Supply of Money in a Developing Economy: A Structural Analysis for India." *Review of Economics and Statistics* 56 (1974): 502–10.

Biddle Papers. Biddle to Webster (April 10, 1833). Washington, D.C.: Manuscript Division, Library of Congress.

———. Biddle to Verplanck (November 19, 1833).

———. Biddle to Hamilton (February 1, 1834).

Bourne, E. G. *The History of the Surplus Revenue of 1837*. New York: G. P. Putnam's Sons, 1885: 40.

Breton, Albert and Ronald Wintrobe. *The Logic of Bureaucratic Conduct*. Cambridge: Cambridge University Press, 1982.

Brozen, Yale. "Minimum Wages and Household Workers." *Journal of Law and Economics* (March 1965).

Brunner, Karl. "A Schema for the Supply Theory of Money." *International Economic Review* 2 (January 1961).

——— and Meltzer, Allan. "Predicting Velocity: Implications for Theory and Policy." *Journal of Finance* 19 (May 1964).

Burger, Albert E. *The Money Supply Process*. Belmont, CA: Wadsworth, 1971: 24–72.

Business Week. "Baker's Plan: No Glitter" (October 19, 1987): 56.

Cagan, Phillip. *Persistent Inflation: Historical and Policy Essays*. New York: Columbia University Press, 1979.

Catterall, R. C. H. *Second Bank of the United States*. Chicago: University of Chicago Press, 1903: 475.

Clark, Lindley H., Jr. "Wigwagging from the White House to the Fed." *The Wall Street Journal* (January 28, 1986): 31.

Clay, H. *Works of Henry Clay*. Edited by C. Coltin. Clay to Francis Brooke (February 10, 1834). New York: A. S. Barnes, 1855.

Cochran, Thomas C. "Did the Civil War Retard Industrialization?" Edited by Gerald C. Nash. *Issues in American Economic History*. Boston: D. C. Health and Company, 1964: 293.

Colberg, Marshall R. "Minimum Wage Effects on Florida Economic Development." *Journal of Law and Economics*. (October 1960).

Cowart, A. T. "The Economic Policies of European Governments, Part I: Monetary Policy." *British Journal of Political Science* (July 1978): 285–311.

Culbertson, John M. *Macroeconomic Theory and Stabilization Policy*. New York: McGraw-Hill Book Company, 1968: 410–11, 545.

Diggins, John Patrick. *The Lost Soul of American Politics: Virtue, Self-Interest, and the Foundations of Liberalism*. New York: Basic Books, 1984.

Dillingham, W.P. Observations to the Author, a former colleague of Professor Dillingham.

Downs, Anthony. *Inside Bureaucracy*. Boston: Little Brown, 1967.

Dwyer, G. P., Jr. and R. W. Hafer. "Is Money Irrelevant?" *Federal Reserve Bank of St. Louis Review* (May-June 1988): 3–17.

Evans, Michael K. *Macroeconomic Activity*. New York: Harper & Row, 1969: 314–15.

Fabra, Paul, "Keynes and the Modern Debasement of Money." *Wall Street Journal* (March 30, 1982): 32.

Fand, David I. "Some Issues in Monetary Economics." *Federal Reserve Bank of St. Louis Review* (January 1970).

Fels, Rendigs. *American Business Cycles 1865–1897*. Chapel Hill: University of North Carolina Press, 1959.

Fisher, Irving. *Purchasing Power of Money*. New York: Macmillan, 1911.

Frankel, S. Herbert. *Two Philosophies of Money: The Conflict of Trust and Authority*. New York: St. Martin's Press, 1977.

———. *Money and Liberty*. Washington, DC: American Enterprise Institute for Public Policy Research, 1980.

Frankel, Jacob A. and Harry G. Johnson, eds. *The Monetary Approach to the Balance of Payments*. London: George Allen and Unwin, 1978.

Frey, B. S. "Politico-Economic Models and Choice." *Journal of Public Economics* (April 1978): 203–20.

Frey, B. S. and F. Schneider. "An Empirical Study of Politico-Economic Interaction in the U.S." *Review of Economics and Statistics* (May 1978): 174–83.

———. "An Empirical Study of Politico-Economic Interaction in the U.S.: A Reply." *Review of Economics and Statistics* (February 1983): 178–82.

———. "Central Bank Behavior: A Positive Empirical Analysis." *Journal of Monetary Economics* (May 1981): 291–315.

Friedman, Milton. "The Keynes Centenary: A Monetarist Reflects." *The Economist* (June 4, 1983): 17–8.

———. "The Role of Monetary Policy" in *The Optimum Quantity of Money and Other Essays*. Edited by Milton Friedman. Chicago: Aldine, 1969: 1–50, 89, 92, 99.

———. "Monetary Policy: Theory and Practice." *Journal of Money, Credit and Banking* (February 1982): 98–124.

———. "Money: Quantity Theory, II." *International Encyclopedia of the Social Sciences*. Vol. 10 (1968).

———. "A Theoretical Framework for Monetary Analysis." *Journal of Political Economy* (April/May 1970): 193–238.

———. "A Monetary Theory of National Income." *Journal of Political Economy*: 323–337.

———. "The Demand for Money—Some Theoretical and Empirical Results." *Journal of Political Economy* 67 (June 1959): 327–51.

———. "A Monetarist Reflects: The Keynes Centenary." *The Economist* (June 4, 1983): 19.

———. "Prices, Income and Monetary Changes in Three Wartime Periods." *American Economic Review* (May 1952): 635.

———. "The Quantity Theory of Money—A Restatement." *Studies in the Quantity Theory of Money*. Milton Friedman, ed. Chicago: University of Chicago Press, 1970.

———. "The Optimum Quantity of Money" in *The Optimum Quantity of Money and Other Essays*. Chicago: Aldine Publishing Co., 1969: 1–50.

Friedman, Milton and Anna J. Schwartz. *A Monetary History of the United States 1867–1960*. Chapters 2 and 3. Princeton: Princeton University Press, 1967.

Gallatin, Albert. Secretary of the Treasury 1801–13.

Golden, D. G. and J. M. Poterba. "The Price of Popularity: The Political Business Cycle Reexamined." *American Journal of Political Science* (November 1980): 698–714.

Goldfeld, Stephen M. *Commercial Banking Behavior and Economic Activity: A Structural Study of Monetary Policy in the Post-war United States*. Amsterdam: North-Holland Publishing Co., 1966.

Gordon, R. J. "The Demand for and Supply of Inflation." *Journal of Law and Economics* (December 1975): 807–36.

H. R. 460, 22nd Cong. 1st Sess.: 363; H. O. Adams, ed. *Gallatin's Writings*. Philadelphia: Lippincott, 1879, III: 336.

H. R. 358, 21st Cong. 1st Sess.: p. 18 and *Niles' Weekly Register*, XXXIV: 154.

Hammond, Bray. "The Chestnut Street Raid on Wall Street, 1839," *Quarterly Journal of Economics* (August 1947): 608–18.

Harding, William F. "State Bank of Indiana." *Journal of Political Economy*, IV (1895): 1–36.

Hart, A. G. "Money: General I."

Hayek, F. A. "The Keynes Centenary: The Austrian Critique." *The Economist* (June 4, 1983): 39.

———. "The Keynes Centenary: The Austrian Critique." *The Economist* (June 11, 1989): 41.

Hazard's Statistical Register I: 328.

Hazard's Statistical Register IV (1841). J. Cowperthaite to N. Biddle (March 23, 1841): 259.

Hebeson, Keith and John F. Chant. "Bureaucratic Theory and the Choice of Central Bank Goals: The Case of the Bank of Canada." *Journal of Money, Credit and Banking* (May 1973): 637–55.

Hein, Scott E. "Dynamic Forecasting and the Demand for Money." *Federal Reserve Bank of St. Louis Review*. (June–July 1980): 13–23.

Hendershoot, P. H. and F. DeLeeuw. "Free Reserves, Interest Rates and Deposits: A Synthesis." *Journal of Finance* 25 (June 1970): 599–614.

Hepburn, A. B. *A History of Currency in the United States*. New York: Macmillan Co., 1915.

Hetzel, Robert L. "The Quantity Theory Tradition and the Role of Monetary Policy." *Economic Review*. (May/June 1981): 19–26.

Hicks, John R. "The Keynes Centenary: A Skeptical Follower." *The Economist* (June 18, 1983): 17–9.

Hirsch, Fred. *Social Limits to Growth*. Cambridge: Harvard University Press, 1977. Second Printing: 122–6, 132–4, 138–43.

Hirschman, Albert. "Rival Interpretations of Market Society: Civilizing,

Destructive, or Feeble?" *Journal of Economic Literature* (December 1982): 1463–84. (Note also Hirschman's discussion of the views of Emile Durkeim on page 1471.)

Horwich, George. "Elements of Timing and Response in the Balance Sheet of Banking, 1953–55." *Journal of Finance* 12 (May 1957): 238–55.

Howe, Daniel W. *The Political Culture of American Whigs*. Chicago: University of Chicago Press, 1979: 78.

Johnson, Harry. "The Ideology of Economic Policy in the New States." D. Wall, ed. *Chicago Essays on Economic Development*. Chicago: University of Chicago Press, 1972: 23–40.

———. "Problems of Efficiency in Monetary Management." *Journal of Political Economy* (October 1968): 971–90.

———. *Macroeconomics and Monetary Theory*. London: Gray-Mills, 1971: 135.

———. "Monetary Approach to the Balance-of-Payments: A Nontechnical Guide." John Adams, ed. in *The Contemporary International Economy: A Reader*. New York: St. Martin's Press, 1979: 205.

Kemp, Jack. "The Renewal of Western Monetary Standards." *Wall Street Journal* (April 7, 1982): 30.

Ketcham, Ralph. *James Madison: A Bibliography*. New York: Macmillan, 1971: 175.

Keynes, John Maynard. *Monetary Reform*. London: Harcourt Brace and Co., 1924.

———. *The General Theory of Employment, Interest and Money*. New York: Harcourt, Brace, 1936: 170–1, 194–7, 380–1. (Discussion in Hirschman, "Rival Interpretations of Market Society.": 1466–8.)

———. "Theory of Rate of Interest." (1937). Reprinted in *Readings in the Theory of Income Distribution*. W. Feller and B. F. Healey, eds. Philadelphia: The Blakiston Co., 1949: 422.

———. *Economic Consequences of the Peace*. London: Macmillan, 1920.

———. "My Early Beliefs." *Collected Writings*. London: St. Martin, 1971–73. Vol. X: 446.

———. *A Treatise on Money*. Vol. I. London: Macmillan, 1930: 3–4, 6, 8–9.

Kidder, R. M. "Nation as Community: A Mixed Blessing for U. S." Interview with Robert Nisbet. *The Christian Science Monitor* (May 26, 1988): 19–20.

Kindahl, James K. "Economic Factors in Specie Resumption: The United States 1865–79." *Journal of Political Economy* (February 1961): 34–5.

Laidler, David and Nicholas Rowe. "Georg Simmel's Philosophy of

Money: A Review Article for Economists." *Journal of Economic Literature* (March 1980): 97–105.

———. Review of Frankel's study in *Journal of Economic Literature* (June 1979): 570–2.

———. *The Demand for Money: Theories and Evidence*. Scranton, Pa.: International Textbook, 1969: 106–97.

Laughlin, J. L. *History of Bimetalism in the United States*. Chicago: University of Chicago Press, 1901: 66ff.

Levy, M. D. "Factors Affecting Monetary Policy in an Era of Inflation." *Journal of Monetary Economics* (November 1981): 351–74.

Lindbeck, Assar. "Stabilization Policy with Endogenous Politicians." Richard T. Ely Lecture. *The American Economic Review* (May 1976): 1–19.

Lippman, Walter. "Letter to William Allen White, June 28, 1937." John Morton Blum, ed. *Public Philosophies Selected Letters of Walter Lippman*. New York: Ticknor and Fields, 1985: 362.

———. Good Society. New York: Grosset and Dunlap, 1943. First published in 1937.

———. Correspondence with John Maynard Keynes (April 17, 1934). (January 9, 1935). (January 31, 1940). (April 2, 1942). (March 23, 1945). (January 2, 1946).

Macesich, George. "Are Wage Differentials Resilient? An Empirical Test." *Southern Economic Journal* (April 1961).

———. *Monetarism: Theory and Policy*. New York: Praeger Publishers, 1983: Chapters 3 and 7.

———. *The Politics of Monetarism: Its Historical and Institutional Development*. Totowa, NJ: Rowman and Allanheld, 1984: 10–2, Chapter 6.

———. "Stock and the Federal Reserve System." U.S. Congress. House Subcommittee on Domestic Finance of the Committee on Banking and Currency. *Compendium on Monetary Policy Guidelines and Federal Reserve Structure* and "Central Banking, Monetary Policy and Economic Activity": 437–54. 90th Congress. 2d Session (December 1968). Washington, DC: U. S. Government Printing Office 1968.

———. "Sources of Monetary Disturbance in the United States, 1834–1845." *Journal of Economic History* (September 1960): 407–34.

———. *The International Monetary Economy and the Third World*. New York: Praeger Publishers, 1981. Chapters 1–3.

Macesich, George and Charles T. Steward, Jr. "Recent Department of Labor Studies of Minimum Wage Effects." *Southern Economic Journal* (April 1960).

———. "Recent Department of Labor Studies": 288ff.

Macesich, George. "Are Wage Differentials Resilient? An Empirical Test." *Southern Economic Journal* (April 1961).

Macesich, George and H. Tsai. *Money in Economic Systems*. New York: Praeger, 1982.

Martin, J. G. *Seventy-Three-Year History of the Boston Stock Market*. Boston: J. G. Martin, 1873.

Mayer, T. "The Structure of Monetarism." *Kredit und Kapital* VIII Nos. 2 and 3 (1975): 190–218, 293–316.

———. *The Structure of Monetarism*. New York: W. W. Norton and Company, 1978.

McCallum, B. T. "The Political Business Cycle: An Empirical Test." *Southern Economic Journal* (January 1978): 169–90.

McDonald, Stephen L. "The Internal Drain and Bank Credit Expansion." *Journal of Finance* 7 (December 1953): 407–21.

McGrane, Reginald Charles. *Panic of 1837*. Chicago: University of Chicago Press, 1929: 190, 207.

Meigs, A. J. *Free Reserves and the Money Supply*. Chicago: University of Chicago Press, 1962. (A. Meigs [1962] discussion on free reserves and the money supply.)

Meiselman, David, ed. *Varieties of Monetary Experience*. Chicago: University of Chicago Press, 1970.

Meltzer, Allan H. "The Behavior of the French Money Supply: 1938–54." *Journal of Political Economy* 67 (June 1959): 275–96.

Minsky, H. P. "Central Banking and Money Market Changes." *Quarterly Journal of Economics* 67 (May 1957).

Modigliani, R. Rasche, R. H., and Cooper, J. P. "Central Bank Policy, the Money Supply and the Short Term of Interest." *Journal of Money, Credit and Banking* 2 (May 1970).

New Monetary Control Procedures. Federal Reserve Staff Study. Vols. 1 and 2. (February 1982). Washington, DC: Board of Governors of the Federal Reserve System, 1982.

New York Spectator. (December 15, 1836). Open letter from N. Biddle to J. Q. Adams on November 11, 1836.

Niles Weekly Register. (March 1, 1834): 9.

Niles Weekly Register X: 20.

Officer, Lawrence H. "The Floating Dollar in the Greenback Period: A Test of Theories of Exchange Rate Determination." *The Journal of Economic History* (September 1981): 629–50.

Paldam, M. "A Preliminary Survey of Theories and Findings on Vote Popularity Functions." *European Journal of Political Research* 9 (1981): 181–99.

———. "An Essay on the Rationality of Economic Policy: The Test-Case of the Electional Cycle." *Public Choice* 37 (1981): 287–305.

Parkin, N. Richards, I. and Zis, G. "The Determination and Control of the World Money Supply Under Fixed Exchange Rates, 1961–71." *Manchester School* 43 (September 1975): 293–316.

Patinkin, Don. *Money, Interest and Prices*. Evanston, IL: Row Peterson, 1965.

———. *Keynes' Monetary Thought*. Durham: Duke University Press, 1976.

Patinkin, Don and J. Clark Leita, eds. *Keynes, Cambridge and the General Theory*. Toronto: University of Toronto Press, 1978.

Peterson, John M. "Recent Needs in Minimum Wage Theory." *Southern Economic Journal* (July 1962).

Pierce, James L. "The Myth of Congressional Supervision of Monetary Policy." *Journal of Monetary Economics* (April 1978). Reprinted in Thomas M. Havrilesky and John T. Boorman, eds. *Current Issues in Monetary Theory and Policy*. 2d ed. Arlington Heights, IL: AHM Publishing Company, 1980: 482.

Pocock, J. G. A. *The Machiavellian Moment: Florentine Political Thought and the Atlantic Republican Tradition*. Princeton: Princeton University Press, 1975.

———. *Virtue, Commerce and History, Chiefly in the Eighteenth Century*. Cambridge: Cambridge University Press, 1985.

———. *The Ancient Constitution and the Feudal Law: A Study of English Historical Thought in the Seventeenth Century*. Cambridge: Cambridge University Press, 1957.

Putman, Bluford M. and D. Sykes Wilford, eds. *The Monetary Approach to International Adjustment*. New York: Praeger, 1978.

Remini, Robert. *Andrew Jackson and the Course of American Freedom, 1822–1832*, Vol. 1. New York: Harper & Row, 1981.

Reports of the Secretary of the Treasury III (1829–37): 678–764; and Comptroller of the Currency for 1876.

———. Circular letter to Depository Banks (May 1837).

———. Vol. IV (1838).

Reynolds, L. G. "Wages and Employment in the Labor-Surplus Economy." *American Economic Review* (March 1965).

Robertson, D. H. *Money*. London: Nisbet, 1948.

Schlesinger, Arthur, Jr. *The Age of Jackson*. New York: Little, Brown, 1945.

Schneider, F. and B. S. Frey. "An Empirical Study of Politico-Economic Interaction in the U. S.: A Reply." *Review of Economics and Statistics* (February 1983): 178–82.

Schumpeter, Joseph A. in *The New Economics*. Seymour Harris, ed. with quote by S. Herbert Frankel. New York: Alfred A. Knopf, 1947: 63–80.

———. *The Theory of Economic Development*. Oxford: Oxford University Press, 1961: 73.

Schwartz, Anna J. "Pennsylvania Banking Statistics" and "New York Banking Statistics." Unpublished manuscripts. National Bureau of Economic Research.

———. "Why Money Matters." *Lloyds Bank Review* (October 1969).

Selden, R. T. "Monetarism" with Sidney Weintraub, ed. *Modern Economic Thought*. Philadelphia: University of Pennsylvania Press, 1976: 253–74.

———. "Velocity of Circulation, III."

———. "Monetary Velocity in the United States." Milton Friedman, ed. in *Studies in the Quantity Theory of Money*. Chicago: University of Chicago Press, 1956.

Selznik, P. "Foundations of the Theory of Organizations." *American Sociological Review* 13 (1948). Reprinted as F. E. Emery, ed. *Systems Thinking*. Harmondsworth Publishers, Penguin Books, 1969.

Shackle, G. L. S. *The Years of High Theory: Invention a Tradition in Economic Thought, 1926–1939*. Cambridge: Cambridge University Press, 1983.

Simmel, Georg. *The Philosophy of Money*. Translated by T. Bottomore and D. Frisby. Introduction by D. Frisby. London and Boston: Rutledge and Kegan Paul, 1977, 1978: 160.

Smith, Lawrence B. and John W. L. Winder. "Price and Interest Rate Expectations and the Demand for Money in Canada." *Journal of Finance* (June 1979): 671–82.

Smith, P. E. "Money Supply and Demand: A Cobweb?" *International Economic Review* 8 (February 1967): 1–11.

Smith, Walter B. *Economic Aspects of the Second Bank of the United States* (Cambridge: Harvard University Press, 1953).

Sumner, W. G. *Banking in the United States*, Vol. I in *History of Banking in All Nations*, 4 Vols. (New York: *Journal of Commerce and Commercial Bulletin*, 1896).

Teigen, Ronald L. "Demand and Supply Functions for Money in the United States: Some Structural Estimates." *Econometrica* (October 1964): 476–509.

The Economist (September 19, 1981): 17–8.

de Tocqueville, Alexis. *Democracy in America*. Garden City, NY: Doubleday, 1969.

Tufte, E. R. *Political Control of the Economy*. Princeton: Princeton University Press, 1978.

U. S. Congress. House of Representatives. H. R. 460. 22nd Congress. 1st Sess.: 363; H. O. Adams, ed. *Gallatin's Writings*. Philadelphia: Lippincott, 1879, III: 336.

———. H. R. 358. 21st Cong. 1st Sess.: 18; and *Niles Weekly Register* XXXIV: 154.

U. S. Congress. Senate. S. D. 16. 23rd Cong. 1st Sess.: 4–5.

———. S. D. 25th Cong. 3rd Sess. I: 13–4.

Vaughn, Karen Iversen. *John Locke: Economist and Social Scientist*. Chicago: University of Chicago Press, 1980.

Weintraub, Robert E. "Congressional Supervision of Monetary Policy." *Journal of Monetary Economics* (April 1978): 341–62.

Williamson, O. F. *The Economics of Discretionary Behavior: Managerial Objectives in a Theory of the Firm*. Chicago: Markham Publishing Company, 1964.

Wooley, J. "The Federal Reserve System and the Political Economy of Monetary Policy." Ph.D. diss., University of Wisconsin, 1980.

Zecher, J. Richard. *Preface to Monetary Approach to International Adjustment*: ix–x.

Index

ABOUT THE AUTHOR

GEORGE MACESICH is Professor of Economics and Director of the Center for Yugoslav-American Studies, Research, and Exchanges at the Florida State University in Tallahassee. He received his Ph.D. in Economics from the University of Chicago. His most recent books include *World Crises and Developing Countries* (1984), *World Banking and Finance: Cooperation Versus Conflict* (1984), *Economic Nationalism and Stability* (1985), *Monetary Policy and Rational Expectations* (1987), *Essays on the Yugoslav Economic Model*, with D. Vojnic and R. Lang (1988), *Banking and the Third World Debt: In Search of Solutions* (1988), and *Monetary Reform and Cooperation Theory* (1989). He is also author of numerous articles in professional journals.